BLACKCARD UNIVERSITY

Real Estate Investing - Sales - Coaching

Are You Ready To Begin Your Journey To Total Freedom?

Join Blackcard University - A 5-year Wealth Building Curriculum

Blackcard University is different.
Get out of the classroom and inti the real world.
Get paid to learn by doing actual real estate deals.
Join Blackcard University's Mi5 Program and learn what it takes to
build wealth and become a millionaire in 5 years.

For more information, go to **blackcardu.com**

Advance Praise For The Ten Commandments of Negotiation

"Stefan is a genius in negotiating. His book *Self Made*, fired me up to achieve even bigger goals. This book is the gold standard for selling. Everything in life is a negotiation."

> —TAMMY KLING, *Best Selling Author, CEO of Onfire Books Leadership Company*

"*The Ten Commandments Of Negotiation* is only for you if you want to be hugely successful in business and life. Stefan Aarnio nailed it. Don't just read it, utilize the proven concepts that Stefan has wedged between these covers."

> —SHAWN SHEWCHUK, *The #1 Results Coach, Bestselling Author*

"We are all negotiating all the time, whether we know it or not. The question you should be asking yourself is: "Am I really any good at it?" If you want to make more money, do more deals, have better relationships, and realize your true potential - get this book and READ IT. I wish I knew as much about negotiations as Stefan does when I was a young punk like him—I'd be way further ahead."

> —DAVE DUBEAU, *Investor Attraction Specialist & Consultant www.DaveDubeau.com*

"Negotiation is one of the most important skills of an entrepreneur and *The Ten Commandments Of Negotiation* outlines a clear path to negotiating success."

> —TONY JEARY, *The RESULTS Guy*™

"Art of the Deal on Steroids! I am privileged to know the author of this exceptional handbook, a man who has proven over and over that he walks his talk and has achieved remarkable success. This isn't another padded ego booster by some wanna-be coach who is trying to feel important; instead, this manual contains a practical guide to the thoughts and reasoning of one who has made this process work majestically for him. I cannot recommend it highly enough. I learned a substantial amount from reading it."

—Robin Elliott, *LeverageAdvantage.com*

"Wow, Wow, Wow! This is an excellent book! I love how honest and candid Stefan is in this book! *The Ten Commandments of Negotiation* is a fantastic tool that will 'up your game' in negotiation guaranteed! Stop getting what society and the world gives you, and start negotiating using the Ten Commandments to get what you REALLY want out of life! This book will pay for itself ten fold within one day of reading it!"

—Paul Kazanofski, *CEO of Revision Homes and TV Personality*

"As a student of negotiation, a competent daily practitioner of negotiation, and as someone who regularly teaches negotiation and sales skills to others, I can say, without reservation, that Stefan has nailed the subject matter of negotiation. He has made this very important life skill easy for all to understand and grasp. The highest paid people in the world are always the best negotiators! I will be ordering several copies and handing them out to my negotiation students as a first read."

—Ross Lightle, *"Canada's Premier Real Estate Coach"*

"In life, you don't get what you deserve, you get what you negotiate. Stefan outlines the most powerful negotiation principles that anyone can use to succeed in business and in life. You can't afford not to read this book!"

—Dan Lok, *The King of High-Ticket Sales, Multi-Millionaire Entrepreneur & Best-Selling Author*

"Negotiation is a game and like any game, you need to know the rules. This book is the rulebook that you need to succeed."
　　—Ross Alex, *Principal, Flipping In Action*

★ ★ ★ ★ ★

"*The Ten Commandments Of Negotiation* is recommended reading for anyone looking to win in business, real estate or life. I made an extra $1000 days after learning one negotiation tactic. This is real world advice, and I use it every time I go to the negotiating table."
　　—Dan Nagy, *Canadian Real Estate Wealth Magazine's Investor of the Year*

★ ★ ★ ★ ★

Negotiation is the Achilles heel of entrepreneurial struggle; life and death, success and failure. Yet business people today barely comprehend the process and rarely acknowledge their weakness in utilizing it. Thankfully, Stefan Aarnio drives an iron stake right through the heart of the negotiating battleground and delivers an arsenal of real life tactics and strategies designed to deliver us ultimate victory.
　　—LES Evans, *Legendary Coach To Celebrities & The Best People In The World*

THE TEN COMMANDMENTS OF NEGOTIATION

STEFAN AARNIO

Clovercroft Publishing

The Ten Commandments of Negotiation

Published by Clovercroft Publishing, Franklin, Tennessee.

Cover Design by Marla Beth Thompson

Interior Design by Suzanne Lawing

Edited by Adept Content Solutions

Printed in Canada

978-1-945507-42-7

Dedication

This book is dedicated to anyone with a hunger, a desire and a passion to get more out of life. You were born destined for greatness.

Everything you want or desire is owned or controlled by someone else and to get it you must negotiate. Opening this book is your first step towards accessing the greatness inside of yourself and the abundance available in the world to those who have mastered the strategies and techniques found in this book.

You are in the right place.

You are Self Made, you are on a journey, and I salute you in the pursuit of your highest and greatest self.

Respect The Grind

Stefan Aarnio

Contents

Foreword

By George H. Ross, Esq.

There is nothing more emotionally rewarding than teaching.

I have been lecturing on negotiation for decades in colleges, universities across the United States and business conferences throughout the world. One never knows who may be in the audience listening to you and what impact, if any, you may have on their lives. I didn't know that one of my speeches would ignite a spark in a young man's mind and change his life forever. That man is Stefan Aarnio who is the author of this outstanding book.

According to Stefan, prior to one of my speeches in 2012, he had no knowledge of the art of negotiation. At that time, he was a relatively inexperienced newcomer to the entrepreneurial world. He lacked skills in two major areas, negotiation and time management.

Realizing the wisdom of my advice, Stefan took it upon himself to become a diligent student of negotiation through real life experiences in real estate dealings coupled with study of techniques from books written by recognized experts in the field. I did the same thing when I was initially developing my negotiating techniques but there was little written on the subject so I learned by trial and error. Had this book existed I would have become proficient much faster and avoided many disappointments resulting from my lack of knowledge.

Throughout my career I have been a chief negotiator and attorney for Donald Trump prior to his presidency. Donald was but one of several renowned, wealthy, successful and prolific real estate investors, developers, and entrepreneurs who made millions as a direct result of utilizing my negotiation expertise.

It is typical for someone to acquire experience through investing and entrepreneurship but it is unusual and commendable for someone to take the time and effort to document their knowledge. I enlightened Stefan in the art and intricacies of negotiation with what I said and wrote. This book is his turn to do the same for the readers of this outstanding work. In my opinion it should be on everyone's "must read" list.

I wish all readers success in their chosen endeavors.

Sincerely,

George H. Ross, Esq.

How This Book Came To Be

"85% of your financial success is due to your personality and ability to communicate, negotiate and lead. Shockingly, only 15% is due to technical knowledge."

–Carnegie Institute of Technology

In 2012 I attended a business seminar in Las Vegas, Nevada where a famous lawyer, George Ross of the Donald Trump organization was speaking. George Ross was in his eighties at the time, and was retired from his legal career but had lived a prolific career as a real estate lawyer. Early in his career, George was hired by the legendary New York real estate investor Sol Goldman and negotiated and transacted hundreds of large commercial real estate deals in New York City. Later in his career, George was hired by young Donald Trump at the age of twenty-seven to negotiate and put together some complex and sizable real estate deals in New York City. As George Ross took the stage he said something I would never forget: "Most entrepreneurs fail because they fail at two major things: time management and negotiation."

George then proceeded to lecture the audience on the fundamentals of negotiation, and of course he had written a book on the subject and had taught at many universities over his lifetime. George was a pioneer teaching at many of these universities because until fairly recently, negotiation was not considered to be a real subject of study.

As a budding entrepreneur myself, I had never considered negotiation to be a study or a skill. As a matter of fact, I considered myself to be a good negotiator at the time and later learned when I began to study negotiation that I was in fact a horrible negotiator. I went on to study negotiation and apply the principles and techniques to my own real estate investment business and achieved great success. Throughout my real estate career, I began to coach and mentor others on their own real estate investment businesses, and I learned that nearly every student under my mentorship was a poor or inadequate negotiator! Unfortunately, in real estate all profit is either found through negotiation or built through construction. As I review the profit and loss statement of my own real estate business, it did not take me long to learn that nearly all of my profits were earned because I negotiated them into the deal. In real estate there is no inherent profit in the business; all profit must be negotiated! As an entrepreneur I had identified a major problem in the marketplace. I had many customers in my coaching business who desired to make a profit in real estate investment and were blind, like I was, to the most important skill of their financial success: negotiation.

Negotiation is something everyone needs, but no one wants. Naming this book and naming this project was a painful process. No one wakes up in the morning to buy a book or program on negotiation. Similarly, we do not want to own a brand-new power drill; rather, we wish to have the hole that the drill produces. We all want the results of becoming a better negotiator without putting in the time, effort, energy, or money to study negotiation.

Herein lies the problem: we have a patient who is sick, he needs to learn to negotiate, but like all medicines, the medicine—the cure—is bitter and unstimulating. The patient would rather eat chocolate, cheese, or candy than the medicine, and rightfully so. After reading many books on "negotiation" I have concluded that negotiation is indeed a boring subject to read about and write about and thus, very few people wish to study it or buy into the idea of studying it. It is my chief aim to make this book exciting and relevant for you because 85 percent of your financial success relies on this: your personality, your ability to lead, communicate, and negotiate. This dose of medicine was created just for you and in the words of Mary Poppins, I will do my best to serve the medicine with a spoonful of sugar.

Your personality, ability to lead, communicate, and negotiate—namely the skills taught in this book—are so important, in fact, that they support your entire financial future! If you have the ambition and foresight to seize and master this skill, over time, your financial future will be brighter than it is today—guaranteed!

The fact that you have self-selected and have chosen to invest in yourself has set you apart from the pack. Eighty percent of books that are bought are never read, so by getting this far you are already in the top 20 percent of achievers. As Woody Allen says, 80 percent of success is just showing up. Thank you for investing in yourself, thank you for committing to your success, and thank you for your commitment to your number one financial skill: the ability to negotiate. Your financial success rests on your shoulders and with the proper study, guidance and care, through negotiation you can have the whole world in your hands.

Respect the grind,

Stefan Aarnio

You Were Born To Negotiate!

"So much of life is a negotiation—so even if you're not in business, you have opportunities to practice all around you."

– KEVIN O'LEARY

Believe it or not, you were born to negotiate. You are able to read these words today because you won your first negotiation. When you were a tiny baby, you were hungry so you cried for your mother's milk. As a natural-born negotiator, you cried—and she fed you. You were born to negotiate, and you won your first negotiation!

As you grew up, you went to school, and negotiating became less acceptable. You were no longer allowed to kick and scream and cry when you wanted to play with a specific toy. You couldn't throw a tantrum to get your way, and, in fact, when you entered grade school, the school system did everything it could to decondition you from your natural-born negotiation abilities.

The school system was designed to create compliant workers, soldiers, and employees, not a society of free-thinking natural-born negotiators. A school with 500 compliant children is easy to manage, not a school of 500 individualistic negotiators, each demanding to get what they want.

In some ways it's a good thing that the school system does not train each and every child to get what they want through negotiation, or society could break down into anarchy. After all, someone does need to push the buttons and pull the levers in the factory. However, you are special. You are special because you are reading this book. You know deep down in your heart that you were born to negotiate and that everything you want is owned or controlled by someone else, and to get it, you must reclaim your natural-born talent of negotiation.

You were born to be a great negotiator, but like riding a bike, you do not come out of the womb ready to ride. You must learn, study, fall down, scrape your knee, and get up to ride again.

Educate comes from the Latin word educare, which means to lead out. This book is here to educate you on the subject of negotiation and draw out the natural-born negotiator hidden inside. You were born to negotiate; seize this skill and claim the life that you were born to live!

The History of Getting What We Want and the Reptile Brain

Everything you want in life is out there in the world, either controlled or owned by someone else. In the Stone Age a tribe of cavemen would go to war with a neighboring tribe, kill them, and steal what they wanted—resources, land, and women. During the rule of the mighty Roman Empire, Romans would wage war with their neighboring tribes and take what they wanted through violence and plunder. In the modern world, it is no longer socially acceptable to kill, wage war, rob, and steal your way to prosperity. Instead we must negotiate to get what we want. In many ways, negotiating for resources or land is a more humane way for human beings to get what they want, and it is certainly less violent than war or plunder. However, negotiation between human beings has always, and will always be, a study of human nature. Human nature is an endlessly fascinating study, and ironically the things that make us human at our best can make us inhuman at our worst. Human nature can appear to be ugly or inhuman because lurking beneath the thin veil of sophistication, civilization, and benevolence lies the brain of a reptile.

A human brain is really not just one brain; it is three brains stacked on top of one another with the most primitive brain at the base and holding all of the decision-making power.

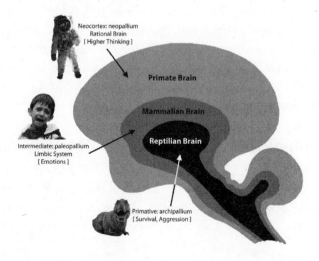

25

The Thinking Brain—The Neocortex

The highest, most evolved, most advanced brain is the thin layer of grey matter at the top of the brain called the neocortex. The neocortex is the thinking brain and the part of the brain that we celebrate and worship with through art, music, poetry, science, and mathematics. The neocortex is the thinking brain that allows us to create, in the words of Plato, the true, the good, and the beautiful, and it also is the part of the brain that constructs lies and ingenious ways to hurt, kill, deceive, and cheat other people. The neocortex is the conscious part of the brain and ultimately the part of the brain that has separated human beings from every other animal on the planet. We are able to think ahead, form complex plans, access the spiritual realm, create and use tools, form large super-tribes, read, write, and build the atomic bomb. Man is the king of all animals because through the use of his neocortex he has been able to transcend the other beasts in the animal kingdom through creativity, planning, and thinking.

The Emotional Brain—The Mammalian Brain

Underneath the neocortex is the mammalian brain, which is less evolved than the neocortex. The mammalian brain is the midbrain, and it drives us to flock and freeze. After the dinosaurs were wiped out, mammals dominated the earth through their warm blood, which allowed them to survive the ice age and form tribes. The mammalian brain is responsible for sheep flocking together into a herd for protection or for hundreds of bison running in a panicked fashion over a cliff and plunging to their deaths. The mammalian brain is the part of the brain that makes humans want to fit in and be a part of a tribe. It's the part of the brain that makes investors sell their stock at an all-time low when market is crashing and it's the part of the brain that makes a home owner freeze and fail to take action when his home is being foreclosed on.

The Reptile Brain—The Decision-Making Brain

Underneath the mammalian brain is the brain of a reptile. The reptilian brain is the base of the human brain and it is only concerned with self-preservation and survival. The reptilian brain is the part of the brain that keeps you alive on a daily basis. It allows you to breathe, eat, sleep, digest food, have sex, and perform basic bodily functions. If you form your hand into a fist and punch the air above you, your reptilian brain is allowing you to attack the air. If you form the same fist and try to punch yourself in the face, your reptilian brain is protecting you from an attack on yourself. The reptile brain is the most important of the three human brains because all decisions must pass through the reptile brain to be carried out by the body.

Since all human decisions and thoughts must pass through the reptile brain to be acted on by the body, man is always on some level, a reptile. He is self-preserving; he is looking out for his needs first. He wants to protect his resources and propagate his genes through the survival of his offspring. No matter what a man tells you his motivation and intentions are, no matter how benevolent or beautiful the ideas, the mission, or the purpose, the reptile brain is always lurking beneath the beauty. No matter what a man says is his motivation, ultimately his reptile brain is preserving him and his interests—not necessarily yours!

Does this mean that all men are bad? Not at all; there is beauty in humanity. There is love, compassion, art, science, altruism, spirituality, charity, generosity, creativity, and a myriad of other positive sides to humanity. However, for the purposes of this book, and for the purposes of you getting what you want, we must understand that beneath the beauty lies a beast. The beast is human nature and the reptile brain. When we peel back the thin veil of civilization, and the thin veneer of beauty, we will see the inhuman side of human nature.

"Talk is cheap, and money buys the whisky" is an old saying that differentiates between beautiful words and ugly actions. Any man can say beautiful things, but ultimately when we watch a man take action, we find out if his actions match his beautiful words. A man's tongue will use his neocortex to paint beautiful lies in your mind, while his reptile brain will show you the ugly truth. This book is about acknowledging the beauty of humanity while trusting the reptile to be a reptile. In the words of Sigmund Freud, "Sometimes a cigar is just a cigar."

How to Read This Book

This book was written to be a study of human nature, and ultimately, the number one skill for handling human nature is negotiation. Every successful political leader, military leader, business leader, or tribal chieftain in history has been a student of human nature, and so are you! You want something, they want something, and your interests may or may not be aligned. You cannot bash their head in with a large rock and take what you want because the days of the caveman are over. In the modern world, we no longer resort to violence and muscle to get what we want. Instead we must grapple with human nature through the strength of our minds and negotiate to win what we want!

This book explores human nature through six parts:

Part I: Why We Must Study Negotiation and Why We Don't Learn to Negotiate In School: They say that a man with a strong enough "why" can bear any "how." Why is the study of negotiation mandatory for your success in the modern world? Also, why is the study of negotiation purposely not taught in public education?

Part II: The Ten Commandments of Negotiation: These ten commandments will serve as a base for successfully negotiating to win what you want in life and in business.

Part III: The Four Phases of Negotiation and the Art of Getting What You Want: This section will show you the proven system and method for navigating and handling any negotiation. All negotiations have the same four phases and escalate in the same way.

Part IV: Thirty Laws of Human Nature: Gambits, Moves and Countermoves: This section outlines specific techniques for manipulating human nature to serve your interests. Times change, empires rise and fall, but human nature and our biology remains the same. By no means is this list complete with all techniques in existence; it is, however a fundamental list of common techniques used by negotiators in the field every day.

Part V: How To Negotiate By Reading Body Language: Learn how to read body language and 58 percent of all communication that is made nonverbally.

Part VI: Eight Elements Of Power And How To Increase Your Personal Power: This section focuses on increasing your leverage in any negotiation and combine types of power to your advantage.

Part I:
Why We Must Study Negotiation and Why We Don't Learn to Negotiate in School

"The whole concept of negotiating is intimidating to many people."
—LEIGH STEINBERG

Reason To Study Negotiation #1:
You Are Entitled To Nothing

"In business and in life, you don't get what you deserve;
you get what you can negotiate"

—Dr. Chester Karrass

In post–World War II, America was left as the heavyweight champion of the world. Germany, France, the United Kingdom, Italy, Russia, and many other countries were left in ruins from the bombs and destruction of total war. America with her great factories, vast resources, technical know-how, and manpower became the only superpower left standing. Economically, post–World War II in the 1950s was boom time: amazing cars were built, beautiful homes were constructed, and the factories that were used to build war machines grew into great industrial companies like Boeing, General Motors, and Ford. These factories became the industrial base of the American economy and provided fantastic jobs, a stable economy, and a fantastic standard of living.

In the 1950s the man of the house worked hard and was the primary breadwinner in the home. One man in America could support a family, own a home, and own a car. In the 1960s, to stay competitive, the same man working for the same company had to work more hours to afford his lifestyle—family, home and car. In the 1970s, his wife had to take on some part-time work to maintain the same family, home, and car. In the 1980s the man and his wife both work full time to maintain the family, home, and car. In the 1990s both the man and his wife worked full time plus overtime to maintain the family, home, and car. In the 2000s up until 2008 with the American economic crash, the man and his wife both worked full time but still didn't make enough money to support their family, home, and car so they subsidized their lifestyle on credit cards.

What happened over the sixty-year period from 1950 until 2010 in America?

The story I offer above is a very simplistic view of the average family in the United States, and it reflects two things (1) The competitive edge that America once had in the world by winning World War II, and (2) The entitlement mentality that has become standard in America from enjoying over fifty years of isolated propserity.

The truth is, the age of entitlement is over. No longer is America the best in the world by default when it comes to industry, medicine, or education. With the proliferation of smart phones and the Internet, the world has become very small and very flat. In the 1950s a business would compete with a few small local competitors, and a local man would competete with another local man for a job. We now live in a world where the business on the corner now competes with local business plus competition in China, India, Germany, the UK, and everywhere else in the world. The same goes for jobs: Where the man in the 1950s would compete with his local companions for a job in a factory or in an office, today that same man in America is competing with workers from all over the world in China, India, Mexico, Brazil, and many other economies.

Over the last sixty years the world has become ultra-competitive, and the world has shifted dramatically. The days of entitlement are over, and we no longer live in a world where local needs are met by local companies. There is no such thing as entitlement anymore because the competition is global, and the competition is fierce!

In the words of Dr Chester Karrass "In business and in life, you don't get what you deserve; you get what you can negotiate."

Over the sixty-year slide from being the "best in the world" to being just another player at the table, America gave ground through negotiations to Mexico, China, Germany, Japan, India, and other leading world producers. The government and big corporations gave away their factories, work forces, intellectual property, and an unbeatable compettive edge in exchange for faster and bigger short-term profits.

To paraphrase a Native American proverb, Only when the last fish has been fished, the last tree cut down, and there is no more clean water to drink or air to breathe, will we realize that we cannot eat money.

The beauty in this Native American proverb is that money is derived from having true value—money itself is of no intrinsic value! The profits came out of the factory, the workforce, the intellectual property, the fish, and the trees. True value is what drives economic prosperity and not money unto itself. The competitive edge was bought and paid for over the years through blood, sweat, and tears. Sadly, what took generations to build was given away in moments through a bad negotiation. Through poor negotiations, bad leadership, and shortsightedness, we gave away our real value and took only money in return. In the words of Henry Ford, per-haps the greatest industrialist of all time, "A business that only produces money is a bad business."

To be competitve in the next 10 years or next 100 years, we must focus on our true value of companies, our products, and our people. We may have the best or we may not have the best, but what is true in either case is that we must negotiate to protect what we have and procure what we don't have. The world has many places to shop and buy, to sell or be sold, and these places are global and easily accessible. The only way to be com-petitive going forward is to negotiate: we must protect our true value and negotiate for the best price and positioning of our products and services on the world stage. The days of entitlement are over.

To receive your bonuses including a free personality assessment, quick start training and a quick start phone coaching session, please visit Xnegotiation.com.

Reason to Study Negotiation #2: Why We Are Not Taught to Negotiate in School

T he schools in the Western world are designed to create subordinate, compliant workers for their industrial factories and militaries. Schools operate Monday to Friday from roughly 9 AM until 5 PM, much like the factories, and that the students must be at their work station when the bell rings much like an industrial factory. Creativity and innovation are not rewarded in this system; instead compliance and subordination are. These student factories—schools—churn out a very specific product: compliant people who wait in line, show up on time, and follow directions. These people are the product of the factory and the by-product of the factory is a society of terrible negotiators. Canada, the United States, Britain, and other Western countries are home to some of the worst negotiators in history because the populations of these countries are conditioned and trained to be compliant to do as they are told. Other countries like China, India, Mexico, Brazil, and Israel have different cultures that are not so compliant, so for the non-Western countries, negotiation is a way of life.

In Western supermarkets, American and Canadian consumers are purchasing meat, fish, bread, and produce at the sticker price—or the advertised price as is socially acceptable in the local culture. On the streets of Mexico, street vendors and Mexican consumers are negotiating for the same meat, fish and produce, and they pay wildly different (and much lower) prices.

As a world traveller myself I notice that a three-taco dinner in Canada is $15 whereas three street tacos in the United States is $3, and in Mexico they can sell for even less. Why do the Canadian consumers pay more? Very simply, Canadians are some of the worst negotiators in the world. The Canadian culture is a culture that values being "nice" and paying what people ask. Very seldom in Canada do consumers negotiate the sticker prices of the goods and services being sold at Walmart. Ironically, Walmart has built its economic success on the fact that they have some of the best negotiators and the strongest negotiating process with suppliers in the world. On one hand, Walmart is an excellent negotiator; on the other hand, the American consumer is not!

In reality, everything is open for negotiation—even the groceries on the shelf at Wal-Mart—but we do not negotiate because it is not in our culture. In reality, negotiation is in our nature; just look at a young child or baby before he has been socialized into the public school system. If the baby is hungry, he cries for mother's milk, and his mother gives him her breast. You are reading this book today because you won your first negotiation—you cried for mother's milk, and she gave it to you! If you did not win that negotiation, you would have died. Children go to the store with their parents and kick and scream for a toy they like. Parents, being the hostages of children, will very often yield to this style of negotiation and will give the crying baby the toy that he wants.

Absolutely everything in life is open for negotiation, but first we must ask. As a world traveller, I often find myself checking in and out of hotel rooms many times a year. Many hotel rooms have two bottles of water on the dresser that have price tags on them that say, "If you drink this water, we will charge your room $8 per bottle." Of course $8 for a 10-cent bottle of water is outlandish so I will call the front desk and ask "Where can I find the complementary bottles of water in my room?" The front desk will reply "Sir, we don't provide complimentary water at this hotel."

I will say "I understand. Where can I find the complementary bottles of water in my room?"

There will be a long silence, and finally I will say, "Can you send me four complementary bottles of water to my room? I am very thirsty, and I don't think these two bottles will be enough." There will be another silence, and the front desk will say, "Yes, sir, we will send some up to you."

Although the hotel is selling bottles of water at $8 apiece, by negotiating I will often get free water and many more bottles of water just by asking. The written word says bottles of water are $8 at that establishment, but in actual fact, you can get what you want complements of the house if you ask the right way because everything is negotiable.

After I receive my complementary water, I will call the front desk and ask for a complimentary robe because I did not find a robe in my room. The hotel will comply and send me a complementary robe up to my room.

At the time of check in I will often ask "What is the best room you can upgrade me to today free of charge?" Very often the hotel will upgrade me just because they have nicer rooms than I have booked sitting vacant and empty. The average cost to operate and clean a hotel room for a night is $18, so it doesn't matter to the hotel if they give me a regular room or a suite. You just have to ask.

On the back of the door in the hotel is a sign that says "Failure to check out by 11:00 AM will result in a $450 charge to your room." Most people who read this sign will try their absolute hardest to avoid a $450 charge and will leave the room vacant by 11:00 AM the next day. The last hotel I stayed at, I called the front desk and asked "What's the latest I can check out today?" The front desk replied, "1 PM, sir."

I then asked "Can I purchase this room on a half-day rate to stay until 5 PM?" The front desk replied, "We do not do half day rates, sir."

"Okay," I replied; "what's the latest I can stay today then, 5 PM?" There was a pause on the other end of the phone and the hotel staff said, "You can stay until 5 PM, sir, at no extra charge."

The sign on the back of the door says that staying past 11:00 AM results in a $450 fee but because I negotiated, I was able to stay in the room until 5 PM at no additional cost.

You may be reading these last three examples about bottles of water, robes, and late checkouts at hotels and think to yourself, "Big deal, who cares?" and I agree with you. These are all small negotiations and small deals, but the point I want to make is that everything—and I mean *ev-*

erything—is negotiable, regardless of what people tell you. You may feel an urge to avoid negotiation or to avoid confrontation, or you may have a fear of asking because your social conditioning tells you to take what you are given. But in reality, absolutely every policy, every price, every custom, every expectation in business or in life is negotiatible if you have courage to ask.

Visit Xnegotiation.com to claim your valuable bonuses.

Reason to Study Negotiation #3: Negotiate or Others Will Take Advantage of You

"Let us move from the era of confrontation to the era of negotiation."

—RICHARD M. NIXON

There are two types of people in this world: those who are good negoiators and everyone else who gets taken advantage. Ever since the dawn of man, humans have been taking advantage of their weaker counterparts. A strong caveman would physically beat up a weaker caveman and rob him of his food, shelter, and women. Today there are laws against the physically strong harming the physically weak, but there is very little protection for the average person when it comes to negotiation. Instead of a big burly caveman knocking on your door to physically beat you up and take your food, we may have an unscruplous insurance salesman knocking on our door to sell us an overpriced life insurance policy instead.

We no longer have bands of raiders circling our towns looking to kill the men, rape the women, and throw the children into slavery. Instead we have predatory bankers who sell mortgages to people that cannot qualify. Instead of raiding your house for everything you own, a predatory banker can foreclose on your home by giving you a badly negotiated loan you can't afford with poor terms and then throw you on the street.

The more things change, the more they stay the same. In the medieval days where you would need to know how to fight off a band of raiders who seeks to plunder your farm, today you need to know how to negotiate to protect your position in life and business.

In my life I have had two parts (1) Life before studying negotiation in which I had a very hard time making my way in the world and (2) Life after studying negotiation in which I began to see success in my life and in business.

What stops the average man from becoming a good negotiator to protect his interests?

(1.) **Cultural Constraints**—If you are reading this book, chances are you come from a culture that is conditioned to avoid confrontation and negotiation at all costs. Where Canadians and Americans are conditioned to pay the full sticker price for everything, Mexican and Chinese negotiators are conditioned to assert their interests and get what they want. Negotiation is either acceptable in your culture or frowned upon.

(2.) **Low Self-Esteem or Low Aspirations**—Along with cultural constraints that prevent many people from negotiating, is the result of further conditioning for most people to have a low self-esteem and set low aspirations for themselves. Studies have shown that most people, no matter how great or poorly they perform in a negotiation, always believe they did the best that they could have. The average man will set his aspiration level low provided there is no outside force telling him to raise his aspiration level. This is why many successful athletes, and entrepreneurs have coaches—to raise their aspiration level.

(3.) **Fear of Hurting Other's Feelings**—Most human beings have a need to be liked and care deeply about what others think of them. Negotiation, when you must assert your position on someone else, could make you or the other side very uncomfortable. We are raised and trained to be "nice" people in the Western world, and even professional real estate agents who derive their entire living from negotiating are hesitant to write low offers on properties for fear of hurting other's feelings and consequently, their own reputations.

(4.) **Unawareness of the Process of Negotiation**—Many people who know they must negotiate may be oblivious to the process and systematic study of negotiation. These people are improvising, and any success they have is pure talent or luck. To study a proven system and follow the process is the only path to sustained success. Luck and talent always fall short of discipline and systematic study and application.

(5.) **Unawareness of the Subject of Negotiation**—Many negotiators do not even know that negotiation is a skill to be studied, learned, and measured. If you do not even know that the subject exists, how can you study it? How can you improve? How can you master it?

(6.) **No Experience in the Field**—Shockingly, we live in a culture in the Western world where people can go through life from the cradle to the grave with very little practical experience as a negotiator. When they buy a car, they pay full price. When they buy a house, they pay within 3 percent of the asking price. Should they need to negotiate for something, they have very little experience to rely on, if any at all.

(7.) **Failure Belief**—Many men and women who succumb to social conditioning from the Western school system believe that failure is fatal, and they terrified of failure. Furthermore, they may believe that anything new they try they will fail at, and this failure belief is major inhibitor to success in negotiating.

(8.) **Lack of Discipline**—Nothing can be mastered without discipline and a steadfast commitment to doing things that are uncomfortable. Negotiation is a skill and process that is frequently uncomfortable and dedicated discipline to the subject is the only way for anyone to become adept or a master negotiator.

(9.) **Fears**—The best version of ourselves is on the other side of our fears. There are six major fears that hold us back from everything we want and they are:

Six Ghosts of Fear

1.) **Fear of Death**—The mother of all fears and the ultimate unknown in life.

2.) **Fear of Failure**—Will keep a negotiator from taking new risks.

3.) **Fear of Poverty**—The fear of losing money or being left in a worse financial position after negotiating.

4.) **Feat of Ill Health**—This fear runs in parallel with fear of poverty, which leads to ill health.

5.) **Fear of Loss of Love**—Fear of losing your mate due to bad decisions.

6.) **Fear of Criticism**—Fear of being criticized for asserting your position in life.

(10.) **Weaknesses**—Our weaknesses rob us of our energy and focus to be successful in any pursuit including negotiation. Although this is not a book on religion, all religions of the world agree that sin is a waste of energy. All human weaknesses can be categorized by the seven deadly sins:

Seven Deadly Sins

1.) **Pride**—The mother of all sins and the thinking that you are better or that your situation is different.

2.) **Greed**—The human emotion of wanting "more." Every human being has a magic number and that number is "more." The most important question you have in a negotiation is, When is enough enough? and stick to it.

3.) **Lust**—The undisciplined emotion of sex in a negotiation is a pitfall that can ruin many otherwise competent negotiators. Very often men will be sent to negotiate with women, and women will be sent to negotiate with men. Sex can take the other side's focus off of the real issues at hand.

4.) **Envy**—The desire to count the other side's money instead of your own will prevent you from winning the negotiation. What you want and what they want are two seperate things. Do not count the other side's money—it doesn't matter.

5.) **Wrath**—When emotions go up, intelligence goes down. Sometimes negotiations can get heated, and wrath takes over. When anger takes over, your chances of winning a negotiation go to almost zero.

6.) **Sloth**—Negotiations take a lot of work, time, effort, energy, and sometimes money to carry out. Many humans avoid negotiating purely because it takes energy—don't be lazy!

7.) **Gluttony**—The human emotion of anything done to the extreme. Although opening positions may be extreme in a negotiation and it's effective to be extreme at times, very seldom can you be successful by being extreme over time.

(11.) **Poor record keeping and research**—Superior negotiators conduct thorough research before entering a negotiation and keep excellent records on their position and the other side. Consequently, poor negotiators keep poor records and do little or no research.

(12.) **Bad trading or no trading**—Poor negotiators typically are bad at trading items and will lose to superior negotiators when trading. Poor negotiators are also bad at selling their position to the other side and creating value in their position.

(13.) **Failure to Understand and Embrace Human Nature**—Understanding human nature and how people work is one of the most important fundamentals for negotiating. You may not know the technical intricacies of how a negotiation works, but you can understand human nature and still be successful. Many of history's most successful world leaders, industrialists, entrepreneurs and military generals who shaped the course of history through negotiation, commerce and war had little technical knowledge of negotiation but instead had a deep understanding of human nature. In many ways a deep understanding of human nature can outweigh all technical skills at the bargaining table.

Visit Xnegotiation.com to claim your valuable bonuses.

Reason to Study Negotiation #4:
All Is Fair in Love and War

"Your political reputation affects how likely allies are to trust you, and what kind of deals they'll offer at the negotiating table. There's also some emotional response in there, so factions do bear grudges. Just like the real thing."

—MIKE SIMPSON

In negotiation, as in war, there are no rules. It might seem kind of ironic that you are reading a book about the rules of negotiation, and it may seem a little comical. There are no rules, but at the same time, there are rules to create order out of the chaos. Negotiation is a chaotic subject with unexpected outcomes and results. Rules in negotiation are often like rules in war in that whoever wins the war makes the rules.

I teach a negotiation class to businessmen and entrepreneurs who perform thirty live negotiations over three days. The students negoiated for ten houses, ten cars and ten pieces of furniture. The houses, cars, and furniture are ficticious but each negotiator puts his own real money on the line at the rate of $5 per negotiation. The winner of the negotiation, the person who gets more of what he wants, gets to take the loser's $5 bet, and when people are negotiating for their own money, the results are fascinating. Over three days, the room of otherwise civilized businessmen wearing their best suits degenerates into an anarchy of lying, cheating, stealing, jumping on tables, slamming doors—and one student even stole another student's play money. To an outsider, the picture I have painted of these $5 negotiators may appear to be an inaccurate representation of humanity. These small-time negoitators were only negoiating for $5 at a time; imagine how they would act negotiating for a $5,000 item or $500,000 item. Would their behavior be magnified with more lying, cheating, and stealing? The likely answer is yes. The way a man treats one dollar is the same way he treats a million dollars.

Throughout history great generals and leaders of men have understood human nature and, subsequently, how to negotiate. The Great Wall of China is visible from space and was suppposidly built to fend of a specific group of raiders called the Huns. The Huns were very skilled mounted archers who would storm into a town or fortification on horseback and fire volley after volley of arrows at their enemies. The Chinese, wishing to keep the Huns out of their territory, built the great wall to keep the Huns out, so they travelled West. At the same time, the Roman Empire was splitting into two smaller empires as it began to decline. The Roman Empire, which formerly ruled all of Europe, was now separated into two smaller empires—east and west. Atilla the Hun was the famous leader of the Huns at the time and was so feared and had such a reputation for brutality that entire towns and cities would surrender as he approached their walls and would pay him tribute of gold and silver to go away without shedding blood. Over the years Atilla was hired by the Eastern Empire to attack the Western Empire and then was hired by the Western Empire to attack the Eastern. Through his mercinary military career Atilla and the Huns became very rich through their people's only industry—war. Along with great riches from sacking towns and intimidating them, eventually the Huns were awarded their own parcel of land that was later named Hungary. By being fearless warriors and having a fearsome reputation, a nomadic people with no industries other than war, the Huns were able to carve a permanent piece of land for themselves out of the landscape of Europe that exists to this day. Atilla the Hun was a great negotiator, and although he used force, intimdiation, and power to get what he wanted, he was able to get the gold, land, and slaves that he wanted from a much larger and more powerful enemy than he was by leveraging his reputation, his skill for diplomacy, and by remaining uncommitted to any one side.

Alexander the Great was another one of history's great negotiators and great military leaders. By age thirty, Alexander had conquered the entire known world and he did most of it through negotiation rather than gory bloodshed and mutilation. Many of the cities that Alexander sacked and brought under his rule were done through peaceful negotiation where Alexander would march his superior army up to the walls of an enemy city and would demand tribute. Alexander had the reputation for being a fearless general and had inherited the best army in the world from his father. He would also brutally massacre anyone who stood up to his demands to make examples of them. By using intimidation and later diplomacy, Alexander was able to assemble the largest empire in the world at the time, and he didn't just build the empire; he was also able to keep the empire together through negotiating with the conquered people. Alexander understood the need to be cooperative with the cities, towns, and kingdoms that he brought under his rule. He would assimilate conquered armies into his army and treat the conquered people well because he knew that he only had enough power to stop small uprisings, and thus he had to negoiate. Alexander knew that he could get what he wanted by giving his people what they wanted, and he was successful up until his early death.

Visit Xnegotiation.com to claim your valuable bonuses.

Reason to Study Negotiation #5:
Win-Win Negotiation Is Dead

*"If you don't focus on yourself, your interests
and your situation, then no one else will!"*

—STEFAN AARNIO

There is an idealisitc concept of negotiation called "win-win" negotiation in which both sides attempt to help the other side get what he or she truly wants. In many ways "win-win" sounds like a great concept, and if both sides can meet their needs, that is ideal. However, in the world of reality, "win-win" negotiation is dead. You have a position and something you want. In contrast, the other side has a position and something they want. You are not responsible for the other side achieving their goals, being satisfied, or meeting their needs. This may sound harsh or insensitive to you, but conversely, they are not responsible for your needs, success, or happiness either. What is most important when negotiating is to get what you want and then end the negotiation by getting out! If you can help the other side, great! If you don't want to help the other side, then fine. What is more important than the other side is focusing on what you want and your interests. If you do not focus on yourself, your interests and your situation, then no one else will!

To receive your bonuses including a free personality assessment, quick start training and a quick start phone coaching session, please visit Xnegotiation.com.

Reason to Study Negotiation #6: Every Human Interaction Is a Negotiation

Negotiation begins the second you come into contact with another human being.

Negotiation is like riding a bike.

When was the last time you did not get what you wanted? And why is it that we *don't* get what we want?

In North America we live in a society that is conditioned to accept what we are given. We are *not* taught to ask for what we want. We are born, grow up, and go to school while serving the system and filling the demands of our teachers, parents, and employers. Nowhere in the system of conditioning are we asked about what we want. We are *not* taught to think about what we want or assert our positions. This failure to identify and go after what we want is a downfall of North American culture and makes us less competitive in business around the world.

In Canada and the United States, we are worried about being polite and not offending the other side. Unfortunately, our success is directly correlated to our ability to have hard conversations. We must become comfortable with being uncomfortable and asserting our position to get what we want.

We pay the highest prices for everything in Canada and the United States relative to the rest of the world, and we pay high prices because we are conditioned to accept what we are given. When we go shopping at Walmart, we pay the sticker price for every item in the store; we don't bother negotiating or asking for a better price because of conditioning. In other countries around the world like Mexico, China, and India, goods and services are negotiated, and it's an accepted part of the culture. Ironically, China, Mexico, and India are becoming some of the most competitive players in the global business arena right now while the United States and Canada fall behind.

To become competitive and get what we want, we must negotiate. Everything we want is currently in the hands of someone else, and the only way to get it is to negotiate.

Most people have problems asking for what we want and getting what we want. We typically get what people give us.

Why?

When you were born you were a good negotiator. When you cried for your mother's milk, she gave it to you. That is why you are alive and able to read this; if you didn't win your first negotiation, you wouldn't be here today. Children and babies understand how to negotiate, they point at something they want and cry and scream until they get it. Somehow in the process of growing up and going through social conditioning we lose our innate ability to negotiate and get what we want.

Why is that?

Every human interaction is negotiation, whether it's dating or trying to get your wife to agree to buying a new house or deciding on a restaurant. If you're trying to get your boss to give you the hot new project or a raise, you will have to negotiate. Everyone wants something.

Every look, every touch, and every sound you make is the beginning, middle, or end of a live negotiation. Positions change over time and may become stronger or weaker depending on the circumstances. For example, it may be impossible to get a date with the prom queen when she's on stage wearing a tiara and a sash surrounded by friends, allies, and admirers. However, it would be much easier to get a date with her two weeks later when she breaks up with her boyfriend and is crying behind the school bleachers alone wearing a dirty pair of sweat pants. Great negotiators know how to manipulate time to their advantage and know that positions change as time moves on, and a stalemate today is a deal tomorrow.

As a graduate of a post-secondary institution and having spent sixteen years in school, I learned many things, but very few important things for getting I wanted out of life. In fact, no one ever asked in elementary school, middle school, high school, or university anything about what I wanted.

"When I was 5 years old, my mother always told me that happiness was the key to life. When I went to school, they asked me what I wanted to be when I grew up. I wrote down 'happy'. They told me I didn't understand the assignment, and I told them they didn't understand life."

—JOHN LENNON

It wasn't until four years after graduating from post-secondary education and in my pursuit of becoming a professional real estate investor did I discover that negotiation was even a subject! I was shocked at the difference between what it took to become a smart negotiator versus what it took to succeed in school and get A's.

To be a good negotiator you must be defiant, know what you want, assert your position, ask, question, challenge, validate, and get what you want. It is a completely opposite skill set from anything taught in traditional schools, and I can see why. The traditional school system was designed in Prussia long ago. In fact, Prussia is no longer a country, but the school system that originated in Prussia still exists. The system was designed to create obedient soldiers and employees, and the last thing that the masters of society want are an army of children who know how to negotiate. If the children knew how to negotiate in schools, there would be riots and anarchy. Best of all, the school system would have to reform because it is an outdated dinosaur that needs to die for our society to move forward. I am not attacking education; in fact, I am a huge supporter of education. Education is one of the most important investments a society can make to elevate itself. However, the current school system does the complete opposite by failing to teach people how to negotiate.

Learning to negotiate is one of the top skills for financial success in the modern world. The average college graduate today in 2016 will change careers on average every four years, and as time passes and technology accelerates, I anticipate that careers will become even shorter. The children of today and of the future will need to be more entrepreneurial than ever, and it is no longer enough to go to school, get a job, work until retirement, and then live while the government and your company pay for your lifestyle. In fact, that plan today in 2016 is virtually impossible. To survive and thrive in the modern world, we are returning to a time that is reminiscent of 1910 where everyone was an entrepreneur and very few people had corporate jobs. There were many micro entrepreneurs—people baking bread, people farming, people making clothes, and so on. And everyone had a small business. This is the age of the small business owner, and arguably the most important skill for business is your ability to negotiate. Without negotiation, the businessman cannot earn a profit or survive.

What is more important than ever in today's market economy are your soft skills: your personality, ability to lead, communicate, and—most of all—negotiate! Regardless of your profession, your career, or your business, learning to negotiate is one of the most imperative skills and one of the most transferrable skills. I thank you for taking the time to invest in yourself and learning this very important skill set!

Visit Xnegotiation.com to claim your valuable bonuses.

Part II:
The Ten Commandments of Negotiation

The Ten Commandments of Negotiation

The more things are different, the more they are the same. There are no two negotiations that are identical; some are complex, and some are simple. Some are long processes that take years; some are short and are done in minutes. What remains the same are the fundamentals and undying truths that form a basis of all negotiations—big or small. They say that professionals practice the basics, whether it's free throws in basketball or long tones when playing the violin or trumpet. Professionals always have a firm grasp of the fundamentals and masters have internalized and implemented them. The following section outlines ten fundamental commandments of negotiation that when followed will likely produce a successful outcome. Over time strong fundamentals and good technique will outperform luck, chance or talent which is how most people attempt to negotiate and ineffective over time. The strongest negotiators win bigger and win more often because they have strong fundamentals and weak negotiators are typically improvising. Studies have shown that no matter how favorable or poorly a negotiator performs in a transaction, he will always think that he did his best. When negotiating, many times you can never know if you could have done better or not, but if you stick to the following ten principles, you will surely be effective in getting what you want.

The ten commandments are loosely based on the top three traits desired by CEOs for top negotiators. Years ago, 150 CEO's were contacted and were asked for the top three personality traits desired for the company's best negotiators. The top three desired traits were indeed surprising:

1.) Personality

2.) Knowledge of human nature

3.) Ability to organize information

The ten commandments as I have written them, can be broken down into those three desirable traits. Of the ten, all of the commandments can be classified into personality commandments, human nature commandments, or ability to organize information commandments. Most books on negotiation are very long and very technical with multiple charts, lists, data, matrices, and so on to make the study of negotiation more complex than it needs to be. If you can obey the ten commandments of negotiation as they are laid out as guideposts toward your negotiation goals, you will be successful more times than not in any negotiation. Conversely, should you fail in a negotiation and not get what you want, it is very likely that you have violated one or more of the commandments to cause the negotiation to fail.

Commandment #1: Get What You Want and Get Out

*"Do not go past the mark you aimed for;
in victory know when to stop."*

—Robert Greene

There once was an American lawyer who took his wife to Mexico for a hot tropical beach vacation. The lawyer and his wife found a sunny spot on the beach. It was a bright clear day, and the sun made the sand very hot to touch. The lawyer's wife noticed a Mexican vendor with beautiful Mexican blankets for sale, and she told her husband that she would like one because the sand was too hot to lie down on.

The man approached the Mexican vendor and proclaimed, "That's a beautiful blanket you have there! How much for the blanket!"

"$20 American dollars, Señor," replied the street vendor.

"I'll give you $5 cash right now," replied the lawyer.

"No, Señor, I cannot give away my blankets for $5, but I can sell you one for $15."

"$15 is too much!" replied the lawyer and he walked back to his wife to tell her that he was going to "get a deal" on the Mexican blanket that she wanted.

As time passed and the couple sat on the hot sand, the Mexican vendor walked by again and the American lawyer offered $8 to the Mexican vendor who countered now at $14. The lawyer, too full of pride, felt that $14 was too much money for the blanket, and he and his wife scorched on the hot sand for a few more hours.

For the rest of the morning and into the afternoon both the lawyer's position and the Mexican vendor's position inched toward each other, and finally the lawyer met his maximum price at $11.25 and the Mexican vendor hit his minimum at $12.50. Neither side would budge, and egos were flaring. The Mexican would not yield, and the lawyer would not give in. Finally the sun went down, and the American lawyer and his wife went home without the Mexican blanket, badly burned and uncomfortable from sitting on the hot sand all day. $1.25 had ruined the beach experience for the lawyer's wife, and the rest of the trip was very uncomfortable for him.

The number one rule in negotiating is to get what you want and get out. Negotiating for negotiation's sake often times doesn't make sense, and in the story of the Mexican blanket vendor, the lawyer showed us a perfect example of winning the battle but losing the war. In the big picture, $1.25 is not a big deal to an American lawyer who is taking his wife on a hot beach vacation and as they say, a happy wife is a happy life, but unfortunatley pride, egos, and competitive nature took over and suddenly the lawyer was negotiating out of ego rather than getting what he really wanted—a blanket and a nice beach experience for his wife. Even though the lawyer had successfully negotiated the blanket down to $12.50 from $20 and essentialy a 37.5 percent discount from the asking price, he failed to get what he really wanted—a happy wife with a nice beach experience and a blanket. Pride is the worst sin of all because it fools us to believe that we are better than others and our surroundings. In all religions of the world, sins are a waste of energy, and pride is the biggest waste of energy of all.

When negotiating remain in control and know when to stop. To be in control of something is to be able to start, change, and stop it. Get what you want and get out is the most important commandment in negotiation. Old Jewish wisdom says, "Count your money; don't count their money."

Commandment #2: Have a Pleasing Personality

"All wealth is of the heart and mind and not of the pocket."

—Pharrel Williams

A pleasing personality that is magnetic and able to capture the hearts and minds of others is one of the most important tools to a skilled negotiator. We typically do business with those whom we like and trust, and in order to have likeability and trust we must have a pleasing personality. Deals, concessions, money, opportunity, big breaks, and so on are always available to likeable, pleasing personalities and are hardly ever available to people with unpleasant personalities.

Ten Ways to Transform into a Pleasing Personality:

1.) **Smile**—Smiling is one of the most powerful and influential things you can do to become pleasing. For one, the act of phsyically smiling influences the brain to think that it is happier than it is and others who see you smiling will typically smile back. Smiling is also a display of power, and it shows that you are not troubled by your situation, no matter how difficult it may be.

2.) **Always agree**—"Yes and"—There are three words that must be removed from your vocabulary today if you wish to have a pleasing personality. These words are killers of agreement that is the basis of all relationships and the momentum that fuels all human transactions. The words that must be eliminated are (1) no, (2) but, and (3) however. These three words kill momentum in a conversation or negotiation and can be replaced with "yes and" or simply omitted altogether for a perfectly pleasing effect. An example of "yes and" in effect is: John says to Bill, "I want pizza tonight", and Bill says, "No, I want spaghetti." By using the word "no," Bill has killed any momentum or agreement that was being built between Bill and John. Instead, Bill could simply say "yes and I want spaghetti." The effect is the same: Bill has asserted his position, but he has done it in a pleasing way that diffuses egos and competition. Similarly, "But I want spaghetti" and "However, I want spaghetti" can also be changed to "yes and I want spaghetti." Using the words "yes and" is very powerful because it validates what the other side has said and then asserts your position. Years ago I had a girlfriend that would get annoyed with me because I would say, "Anyways" after most of her statments, and she would get mad because the use of "anyways" did not validate her position. I knew a very charismatic radio host who never used the phrase "anyways" and instead would say, "with that being said," which would create more momentum and agreement. In the words of Dale Carnegie, "The only way to win an argument is to never have one" ring true today. Do your best to keep your negotiation from degrading into an argument by always agreeing and using "yes and" no matter how adversarial or opposite your interests are.

3.) **Tone of voice**—Studies have shown that 58 percent of communication is body language, 33 percent is tone of voice, and only 8 percent is words spoken. When communicating, tone of voice is extremely important because, according to Jordan Belfort (the Wolf of Wall Street) there are twenty-nine types of tone, and having the appropriate tone for the situation will convey the right message. In personal transactions, tone of voice is very important; over the phone there is no body language so tone of voice is 80 percent of all phone communication! To become likeable you must master the tone and sound of your voice.

4.) **A good handshake**—In business and in life more deals are done with handshakes and honor than any other method. Yes, most deals should be done with contracts, paper, and lawyers, but in reality, most deals are done verbally with handshakes first and are papered up later. Handshakes are an extension of having good body language, and in many parts of the world people will trust you or distrust you depending on your handshake. Handshakes are cultural, however, and there is no one perfect way to have a handshake in all situations all over the world. Find out what would be appropriate in your situation and use your best judgement on how to shake the other side's hand.

5.) **Dress up and be well groomed**—They say the fastest way to increase your income is to get a makeover. For men and women, it always pays to be dressed up and to be dressed one notch above the other side. In the words of Coco Chanel, "You can never be overdressed or overeducated." People value well-dressed and well-groomed people and are more likely to accept your position or proposal by being well presented. Years ago one of my mentors ran an experiment in a room of 500 people where each person in the room was to ask the other 500 participants for money. The two men that raised the most money were hotel staff wearing suits. People are conditioned to accept the authority of a well-dressed and well-groomed man or woman. Being well-dressed and well-groomed even translates into the animal world where alpha animals are better groomed than betas and omegas. If you want to be liked, be well-dressed and well-groomed.

6.) **Have unbreakable integrity**—Years ago I had the priviledge of being able to study with a billionaire by the name of Bill Bartmann. Bill was a student of human nature and believed that the most powerful thing a person could do was to do exactly as they said they would. If Bill had a meeting at 3:00 PM in the afternoon, he would show up exactly at 3:00 PM to maintain perfect integrity. Integrity to Bill meant that what he said happened and he knew it was rude to show up at 2:58 PM, and it was rude to show up at 3:01 PM. His personal power and power in his negotiations came from being directly on time and delivering exactly what he said he would deliver. To have a pleasing personality, your word needs to be able to print $100 bills: what you say happens. People love to deal with other people of integrity, and people of integrity consequently make more money. Years ago when I was a musician I had a very low income and also had low integriy. The things I said I was going to do didn't happen. When I began to turn my life around, one of the quickest ways that I increased my income and success in life came from increasing my integrity—what I said I was going to do happened, and all parts of my life became better. Your word is either truth and can be exchanged for gold, or it is hollow and worth nothing—you decide what your word is worth.

7.) **Have a sense of humor**—Nothing diffuses a tense negotiation like a sense of humor. Everyone loves to laugh, and laughing stimulates the emotion of joy in the brain. Dealing with people is always an experience and people will pay a premium (give you concessions in a negotiation) for an enjoyable experience. Do your best to entertain and create humor out of intense situations. You may not always agree with the other side, but at least you can laugh together and enjoy the experience of disagreeing. Humor is so highly valued with people that women who are looking to date men put it as one of the top traits that they are looking for in a mate. In addition, consider that some of the highest paid people in the world are comedians. To become funnier and more likeable, study some of the great comedians of the world for material and delivery.

8.) **Find commonality**—We like people who are like us. Relationships are based on agreement, and finding commonality is an extension of agreement. Do you both love fishing? Do you both like travelling? What is something that you can agree on to create momentum and likeability in your negotiation? The more you have in common before getting down to business, the more social capital you will have to draw on when you need to assert your position or ask for concessions.

9.) **Positive mental attitude**—There are two types of people in the world "yes we can" people and "no we can't" people. Everyone prefers to work with a "yes we can" person, and in the world of business and life, "yes we can" people typically get more done and make more money than the "no we can't" people. In any negotiation, transaction, or relationship, an attitude of sincerely wanting to bring everything to a positive conclusion is worth its weight in gold and certainly makes you a more pleasing person to deal with.

10.) **Harnessed sexual energy**—Sexual energy is the most powerful energy human beings have, and it is essentially all of our creative and actionable energy. Consider an aggressive, dominant bull with raging testosterone. The bull will fight and challenge you for territory because he is a highly sexed beast. Consider the same bull if he is castrated and his testicles are removed: he then becomes an ox and loses all drive, aggression, and much of his attractiveness to his opposite sex. In Napoleon Hill's *Think And Grow Rich*, Hill talks about a concept called "sexual transmutation" in which sexual energy in a person is harnessed for creative energy and personal magnetism. If you study top performing salespeople and influencers, you will notice that they are highly sexed individuals. Much of being magnetic and likeable stems from having sexual energy and magnetism that attracts others to your cause. Part of being magnetic and having a great deal of sexual energy comes from being in shape, having good posture, wearing clothes that complement the body, and participating in the act of sex sparingly and only with a partner that you are in love with.

Commandment #3: Prepare Diligently and Collect All Information

To be a great negotiator is to be a collector and organizer of information. In many ways negotiation is like war in that the bigger army usually wins. In negotiation, it isn't a battle for land or a battle for conquest; instead it is a battle for information. The side that collects more information and organizes it in a better way is usually the winner. Consider a company like Facebook: in 2016 Facebook is worth billions and billions of dollars because they are a company that stores complex information on hundreds of millions of users. The information they have is stored and colleted in a brilliant fashion, and they are able to sell that information to companies around the world so that those companies may negotiate with Facebook's users to buy their goods and services.

Maybe you aren't a high tech negotiator like Facebook, but you still want to be an organized collector of information. In my real estate business, I carry a black book with me. This is a small book that records things I do daily in the front and in the back collects information on real estate deals and negotiations that I have had in the past. In a few seconds I can recall information that was said or offers that were made on any previous deal including names, phone numbers, prices, positions, and so on. And the other side is usually not so prepared. Recording information and keeping good records is key to winning in business and life as a negotiator. I strongly recommend you get a black book to record all of your negotiations.

Commandment #4: Know What You Want and Have Clear Written Goals for Each Negotiation

O ne of the fundamental problems with being human is that we do not know our own minds. The human mind is more powerful than the most powerful super computer on the planet, and at any given time we are using 10 percent or less of our brainpower. Since our brains are so big and powerful, oftentimes our minds can wander and float during a negotiation, and we can lose sight of our original position and what we originally wanted.

I recently bought a luxury condo to fix and sell in my local market for fifty-seven cents on the dollar. The condo was owned by an old lady in her nineties and was outdated on the interior by fifty years. After negotiating a price of $288,000 on a condo that is worth $500,000 fixed up, my eye caught a beautifully carved antique dragon chair. Next thing you know, I was back in the condo weeks later negotiating to buy the dragon chair. Suddenly, I was buying a ten-chair dining set with large dining table, a full buffett, a china cabinet, an assortment of other chairs, king and queen chairs, and an antique settee along with a slew of other antiques that I wasn't planning on buying. I bought all of the lady's antiques for $4,000, which I believed to be a bargain, but when I took the antiques to be reup-holstered, I got a bill for $9,500. I went in to buy a condo to fix and sell for profit and the next thing you know, I was buying $13,500 of antiques. My mind wandered from the condo to the antiques, and this commonly hap-pens in negotiations if we do not have clear written goals and outcomes for each negotiation.

You will see this all the time in real estate, auto sales, or furniture shopping when a customer comes into the store to buy one thing and walks out with another. We do not know our own minds, and the only way to tame the mind is to get your original thoughts written down on paper and stick to the original plan.

Commandment #5: Gather All Information Before Making an Offer

O ne of the pitfalls most negotiators have is that they make an offer too soon before collecting adequate information. At the base of every negotiation is motivation and self-interest. Oftentimes the other side will not reveal their true motivation and self-interest, and there must be a certain amount of information collected before you can make an educated guess on the true underlying motivation and self-interest of the other side. Eighty percent of your time spent in the negotiation process should be used on collecting information with the other 20 percent spent on making an offer and closing the deal. Too many novice negotiators ruin their chances of winning a negotiation by making an offer too early with inadequate information. Information is power and the key to gaining momentum and leverage for your position.

Commandment #6:
Always Present an Offer of Greater Value

When making your offer to the other side, there is always a certain amount of salesmanship required to frame your offer in the right way. What intangible value are you bringing to the table so that your offer isn't just about the cold hard dollars and cents? What relational value can you bring to the table? Is there opportunity for more business in the future? Are you solving a problem for the other side? Are there extra bonuses that they will get by signing today? How can you create extra value and present your offer with greater value even though your offer will be at no greater cost to you? All value is intangible, so find a way to create intantible value for your offer that goes beyond dollars and cents.

Commandment #7: Do Not Give Concessions Freely

Nothing in this life is free; anything of value costs time, money, effort, or energy. Once you have made your offer, you must never give away concessions freely, or the value of your position may collapse. There is a metric in negotiation called the rate of concession, and usually the person who gives the biggest concession first ends up being the loser, so when you make a concession, make it small and always ask for something in return. Remember that concessions don't have to be fair, and they don't have to be on a 1:1 basis. Who says you cannot ask for seven items in return for one concession? Fairness is an ideal created for schoolchildren in the protective bubble of a government school system. In reality, there is no fairness, and when you make trades, there is no reason for you to be fair.

Commandment #8 Take What You Want, Give What They Need

O bey the Rolling Stones' principle: "You can't always get what you want, but when you try sometimes you get what you need."

Between needs and wants is a vast chasm of possibilities. As a principle of negotiation, you must take what you want and give the other side what they need. The other side will always open with their position, which will be filled with wants—things that would be ideal to have. If you peel back the layers of the onion you will find that most of the things that the other side asks for are not as important as a few key positions. Separate their needs and wants clearly and aim to give them what they need while you take what you want. Ultimately, the side that gets their needs and wants met simultaneously is the side that ends up as the winner in any negotiation.

Commandment #9: Obey the Laws Of Nonlinear Time

Understand that time is nonlinear when negotiating and that time can freeze, break, speed up, slow down, and go backwards when negotiating. Negotiations do not always move forward in a linear fashion. They can go sideways, backwards, faster, or slower, and if you understand how to manipulate time and apply time pressure on the other side, you will have an advantage over the other side, much like a general in warfare who understands the terrain of the battlefield. Manipulate time as you see fit and make them play your game when it comes to time.

As a rule, when they want to go fast, you go slow. When they want to go slow, you go fast. Be unpredictable with your use of time and apply pressure when necessary. Most concessions, including the biggest concessions, come out when one side is under a time crunch. When time is limited, people generally make emotional decisions instead of rational decisions.

Use of broken time can be extremely effective in all types of negotiation. If you are at an impasse or a deadlock or if the negotiaton is just getting too intense, you can break the negotiation and resume at a time that is advantageous to you. Time affects all sides differently in a negotiation, and if you can manipulate it to your advantage, you will have the leverage and power to win.

Comandment #10: Become a Student of Human Nature and Irrationality

All great leaders in history have been students of human nature and so are great negotiators. If you want to be an effective negotiator, you must become a student of human nature and understand the irrationality behind most human decisions. Most human behavior makes very little logical sense and is based on emotion rather than rational logic. If you can exploit the irrational side of humanity you will not only become a stellar negotiator, but you may also become rich in the process. Why is red lipstick a best seller and not green lipstick? Why do most people want to buy a new home in the spring? Why do people spend top dollar on the newest fashionalbe clothes only to discard them into the trash or Goodwill twelve to eighteen months later? All of these things are irrational behaviors that people reinforce with logic. Even large companies, stocks, and real estate have an irrational human side to them. Become a master of human nature and find comfort in the irrationality and senselessness that people use to make decisions and expoit these pitfalls for your own gain. Where there is irrationality, there is profit, and it is your duty to capture as much of those irrational profits as posssible.

Part III:
Three Steps to Negotiation and the Art of Getting What You Want

Three Steps to Negotiation and the Art of Getting What You Want

Ninety percent of businesses fail in the first five years of operation, and of the remaining surviving businesses 90 percent of the survivors fail in the second five years of operation. Businesses fail for any number of reasons, but many of these businesses lack systems to make them successful. Consider a famous hamburger chain like McDonalds. McDonalds is a global hamburger juggernaut that is run mostly by teenagers. McDonalds is able to run a global business with teenagers all over the world selling and packaging burgers on nearly every street corner because the system is so effective. In negotiating, most people fail because they are not following a system to help them succeed.

The United States and Canada are home to some of the worst negotiators in the world. We live in a part of the world that fails at negotiation because negotiation is frowned upon in our culture. Furthermore, we have a school system that conditions people to comply and obey instead of defy and negotiate.

Here are a few reasons why Western culture fails at negotiation and then we will explore a system to create negotiation success:

Ten Reasons Why We Fail At Negotiation

1.) **Polite culture**—In the Western world, we do our best to be polite and comply with other people's desires and wishes. Western culture does not look favorably upon people who are impolite or people who assert their own positions and interests on others. In many ways, even the act of asking is looked upon as rude. In other cultures around the world, such as an Arabic culture, it's rude to avoid negotiating.

2.) **Accept the written word**—Children are sent to school from a young age in Western culture to learn to read and write and later obey the written word. At the store in the Western world, if tomatoes are $3, we will just pay what exactly what the sign says. We will not ask the clerk at the checkout desk for a discount, and we typically will not call in the management of the store to ask for a discount. In other parts of the world and in other cultures it's customary to negotiate on everything, and the asking price is not expected to be the paid price.

3.) **Accept authority figures**—In the Western school system we are taught to obey and comply with authority figures so that when we are older, we will comply with the military, police, and government. We are conditioned from a young age to listen to authority and accept authority as truth. In reality, authority is manufactured, and everything is negotiable whether we are dealing with an authority figure or not.

4.) **Not aware we can negotiate**—The Western world has been organized and streamlined for an ease of use in commerce, and we typically expect to pay whatever the asking price is. The vast majority of the population is not even aware that they can negotiate on items that they pay for every day. Years ago I asked my assistant to book a hotel conference room for an event I was putting on. The price was unacceptable to me, and I told her to call back and demand that we get the same hotel room for half price and that we were willing to book the room every month one year in advance. My assistant was unaware that we were able to ask for such a discount and secure such a discount merely by making a proposal. Everything in business and life is negotiable, and if you don't check prices for validity or flexibility, you are likely paying too much.

5.) **Don't want to offend**—In the same vein as worrying about being impolite, we also do not want to offend the other side when negotiating. When asserting our position, we may come off as offensive to the other side if our position is far away from theirs. The reality of people is this:

a third love you, a third hate you, and a third don't care. If you want to make an omelet, you have to break a few eggs. To get what you want out of life and business, sometimes you will need to offend someone. If your proposal to get what you want is offensive, then that is too bad the other side is offended so easily. There is only one way to get what you want in life, and that is to ask! In contrast to offending people while negotiating, it is often best to pick your battles. There are times where it makes sense to negotiate and times where it's best not to bother for practicality's sake.

6.) **We want to be liked**—In the Western world we grow up with a false belief that everyone should like us and that we should like everyone. In real estate I often write low offers on properties that reflect the condition and true value of the bricks, the sticks, and the dirt that I wish to buy. Realtors that work for me are often worried that the other side will not like them and the realtor on the other side of the transaction is worried that their client, the vendor, will not like them if they present a low offer. In the Western world we get too emotional about wanting people to like us. The truth is most people don't care about you at all or even think about you, and some people will not like you no matter what. Get over it and grow up.

7.) **We want to please other people**—For some strange reason we are conditioned in the Western world to want to please others. Not everyone knows the formula for success, but the formula for failure is certainly trying to please everyone. In the pursuit of getting what you want, you will displease people who have interests that are not aligned with yours. You must have enough self-esteem to assert your position and not be worried about whether or not others are pleased with your position.

8.) **We typically don't negotiate**—Another reason for failing in negotiation is that we simply don't negotiate at all. In the USA and Canada we are trained by the school system to avoid negotiating. Immigrants who are born outside of America are three times more likely to become millionaires than native-born Americans because they come into our culture with nothing and must negotiate for every single gain in their lives.

9.) **We don't practice**—Anything worth doing is worth doing well. To become great we must practice. To fail to practice is to fail at becoming great.

10.) **We don't' study**—Negotiation is a study much like science, mathematics, English, or music. It is a deep, rich study full of human nature, value trading, and math and is both an art and a science. If you want to become a successful negotiator, you must study!

Negotiation Is a Skill like Riding a Bike

No one is born knowing how to hop on a bicycle and ride down the road. Over time through trial and error, one learns to ride a bike. The same is true for negotiation. No one is born with the tools, techniques, and strategy to handle complex negotiations, and reading books can only get you so far. To become an effective negotiator you must go out and really do it in the same way that you learned to ride a bike. Get on the bike and pedal until you fall off. An ancient Japanese proverb says "Fall down seven times, get up eight," and the same applies to bike riding and negotiation. You will fall down, you will get it wrong, you will screw it up, but it's the only way to learn. You cannot learn to have sex from a book, and you cannot learn how to negotiate purely from a book. You must get out there and do it!

Four Indirect Ways To Become A Better Negotiator

According to *The Art of Negotiation*, a Harvard Business School publication, negotiation is similar to the following four disciplines: jazz, chess, improv acting, and war. As I began to study negotiation years ago I also found, as I began to teach others, that I was a natural negotiator. Coincidentally, I was also a professional jazz musician for a few years in my early twenties, an avid chess player, a natural born improv actor, and a student of war and history. In many ways, my interests and skill sets over the years directly contributed to my abilities as a negotiator and here is why:

Jazz
Jazz is a type of music where four or five musicians will walk into a room not knowing what they will play. They will start playing a song together and will typically end the song together, but the entire art form is fluid, and each player is playing off one another. Jazz musicians will spend years of their lives practicing rudiments, scales, chord changes, and melodies and will practice for hours outside of the stage to be able to freely impro-

vise on their mastered instruments. In many ways, jazz musicians are the most skilled musicians in the world because they have the technique and abilities of a classical musician while being able to spontaneously compose music in real time relative to the other players in the group without rehearsal as a group prior to a gig.

In many ways, jazz musicians are negotiating with sound. They know the song is going to start at a certain time, and they will end together, but what happens in the middle is one big negotiation.

Chess

Chess is a discipline that is very similar to negotiation because it has two human sides that work against one another to achieve two opposite goals. In the end, there is a winner and a loser and there are negotiation terms that are borrowed from chess. In chess there are gambits, which come from the Italian word *gambetto*, which means to trip. Each chess player will know a series of gambits that they will use on the other side to gain a time advantage or positioning advantage. Fittingly, in negotiation, we use gambits to gain a time advantage or positioning advantage over the other side.

Furthermore, in chess, you can see the irrational human nature that takes place as both sides feel the pressure. You may think that the players are playing rationally, but at a certain point, one side will crack under pressure and do something irrational, which will give the other side an advantage.

At the highest levels of chess the game is played so well that the only way for one side to win over the other is to wait for a mistake to be made. The same applies for negotiation. If you want to become a better negotiator, become a better chess player.

Improv acting

Improv acting, like jazz, is an art form where four or five people in a group will start of on a riff or an idea and will have to carry out that idea to a conclusion. There are few rules in improv acting other than "yes and," and what is significant about the phrase "yes and" is that as an improv actor you must keep the reality of the set alive. To agree with another actor and use "yes and" will keep the momentum of the set alive. If you disagree with another actor about a new idea coming into the frame, the entire show will collapse. Negotiation is extremely similar to improv acting because it is often more powerful to keep the energy and momentum by using "yes and" over creating disagreement and adversarial feelings of using "no, but, or however."

War

All is fair in love and war. The same applies for negotiation. In negotiation the same rules that apply to war apply to you in the pursuit of getting what you want. Buyers are liars and sellers are liars, and when it is your interest against their interest there are no rules, no ethics, and no morals. Everything is fair, and typically winning is everything. Deception is power in that covering your position is important, and both sides in a negotiation will use leverage and power to their advantage.

It may seem dark to embrace negotiation with the same rules as war, but understand that human nature is dark, and with adversarial interests and resources at stake, you are often dealing with the reptile brain, which can bring out the worst rather than the best in people.

The #1 Goal of Negotiation

Often in a negotiation emotions can flare, and egos can take over. You can lose sight of what you originally were negotiating for and can lose perspective completely. However, if you keep your number one goal in mind, you can keep perspective no matter how strange the negotiation becomes. The number one goal of negotiating is:

- NOT to beat up the other side—Negotiation is not about having power over the other side or beating them up or making them feel bad.

- NOT to take every dollar off the table—You don't need to squeeze every last dollar off of the table to the point of getting them to resent you. There is a point where enough is enough.

- NOT to come out ahead—Counterintuitively you may have negotiations where you lose the battle but win the war. Maybe you are giving out a loss leader or maybe you temporarily are set back but will get ahead later. You don't always need to come out ahead.

- NOT to find a win-win relationship—Win-win is something that doesn't really exist and doesn't really make sense. Yes, you can align interests, and yes, you can both get a favorable deal, but you do not always have to make win-win your priority.

- NOT to stay friends or be friends—relationships are great until they aren't. Every relationship has a lifespan and giving up your position on the premise of having a long-term relationship probably isn't good for you. If your interests aren't met in the relationship, then it wasn't a good relationship anyways.

- To "get what you want and get out" is your number one goal in negotiation, and you must never lose sight of what you truly want. Once you have what you want when negotiating, it is time to make a deal and get off the negotiating table. It doesn't matter what the other side gets; get your items and get off the table. Avoid counting the other side's money and obey the old Jewish wisdom: "Count your money, don't count theirs." Be unemotional about what you want, know what you want, and stick to it, no matter what happens during the negotiation or no matter how dramatically the positions change.

Three-C Negotiation—Collect, Clutter, Close

To paraphrase Albert Einstein, "Anything that you understand is simple; if you can't make it simple, you don't understand it." Three C negotiation is very simple: it's a three-step process, and Three C works as a framework for any negotiation, no matter how big or small, simple or complex.

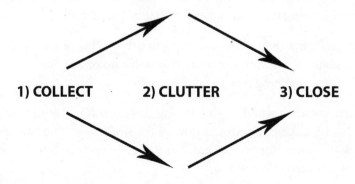

1) COLLECT   2) CLUTTER   3) CLOSE

Phase 1: The Collection phase—Questioning

In the collection phase, the negotiation expands like a crescendo as you collect information by asking the other side questions. The negotiation expands as the possibilities expand while you gain more and more information. Eighty percent of your time in the negotiation should be spent in phase 1.

Phase 2: The Clutter phase—Raising Issues and Making an Offer

In the clutter phase, you have gathered enough information to make an offer. It's extremely important that you do not rush the collection phase and only make an offer when you have an adequate amount of information. When you make your offer you will raise issues or pieces of clutter that you will likely trade away as the negotiation persists. During the clutter phase, the negotiation has expanded because it contains the highest number of possibilities in the clutter phase, and in the middle the negotiation can go in any direction, depending on how the two sides play their cards.

Phase 3: The Close phase—Closing in on What You Want

In the close phase, the final phase of the negotiation, we trade away the pieces of clutter and the issues that we do not really want for the items that we truly want. If you have done a great job of collecting information and raising issues through the clutter phase, then closing in on what you want will be relatively easy. The more preparation you do in phase 1 and 2, the easier phase 3 will be.

The Benefits Of Following The 3C Process

1.) We get what we want—This process will give you the maximum chance of getting what you want in the close phase if you do a good job of collecting information and creating clutter in your offer.

2.) We don't have to give up everything to get it—This process will maximize the items you can give away that will minimize your chances of giving away something that you really want.

3.) The negotiation will flow—Following this process will minimize your chances of breaking the natural flow of the negotiation. Novice negotiators do things in the wrong order and may have to backtrack, which always hurts credibility.

4.) We will know where we are in the process—By having a simple three-step process of collecting information, creating clutter with an offer, and closing in on what we want, we will always know where we are in the process. You are either in phase 1, phase 2 or phase 3.

5.) Maximum leverage—This process will give you the maximum leverage when making an offer because you will have adequate information plus a good deal of commitment from the other side during the collection phase before maximizing your leverage with a strong offer with many issues raised.

Pre-Negotiation Phase—Step 0 Preparation

Of course, every three-step process has a preliminary phase that takes place before step 1, and that is step 0.

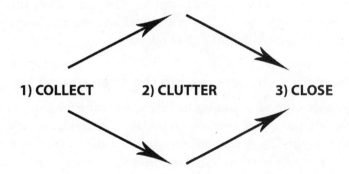

1) COLLECT   2) CLUTTER   3) CLOSE

He who is more prepared for the battle is usually the winner, and in the real world preparation beats experience when done right.

Know Your Enemy

To paraphrase the famous book *The Art of War* by the legendary Sun Tzu:

A warrior who knows himself and knows his enemy will be victorious in every battle.

A warrior who knows his enemy but does not know himself will have one defeat for every victory.

A warrior who does not know himself and does not know his enemy will be defeated in every battle.

To be prepared is to know yourself and to know your enemy and if you are adequately prepared, success will be ensured every time. Most novice negotiators are completely unprepared. If you are going to spend 80 percent of your time collecting information in the 3C process, you want to spend 80 percent of your total time preparing for your negotiation and only 20 percent in the 3C process.

In many ways, preparation before going into battle is more important than the way that the battle is fought and won. In war there is a term called "the fog of war," which is a description of what happens once the troops get onto the battlefield. Once the troops are on the field, anything can happen and the "fog of war" takes over. If the troops are well prepared, they will be victorious; if they are ill prepared, they will die or be captured. If you are adequately prepared for your negotiation, then you minimize the chances of the "fog of war" taking over and losing your position once you go live against a live opponent.

Key Steps for Success during the Preparation Phase:

Step 1) Determine what you want: When preparing for a negotiation you must determine what it is that you actually want so that you can capture it and get out. Ideally you want to write down the exact outcome that you want to achieve in your black book prior to entering the negotiation just in case you lose perspective.

Step 2) Decide what you are willing to give up: In contrast to what you want to achieve by negotiating, you must also determine what you are willing to give up to take that which you want. In any negotiation or transaction there are typically *price* and *terms*. An optional approach can be "your price, my terms" or "my price, your terms" Are we willing to give up on your price? Longer delivery? Financing options? Deposit sizes?

Your preparation will have the most power, validity and weight if it is written down in your negotiation black book beforehand.

Step 3) Determine your non-negotiables: After determining what you want and what you will give up, you must also determine what is nonnegotiable in this transaction. Which points are you going to stick to no matter what? What are you willing to deadlock over and walk away?

Step 4) Anticipate the other side: Next, you must try to anticipate what the other side wants the most and what they are willing to give up to get it.

Step 5) Research the other side: Do some research on the other side. Do you have the names of the people involved? Who will you be speaking to? Do you know about the company and organization you are involved in?

Easy Tip: Google everything. If you need information on the people and parties involved in the negotiation, the easiest thing you can do is google the other side, the address of the property you are buying, or the companies involved in the process. Google is extremely powerful and a luxury we have today that previous generations couldn't take advantage of. It's amazing what you will find on google. For example if you google a property address, within seconds you will know if it was a marijuana grow op, if a sex offender lived there, if a murder has taken place in the home, or if it was a meth lab. Google is extremely powerful—use it!

Besides google you can look up other records, make notes and bring notes into the live negotiation. The more information you have, the better.

Your #1 Negotiation Tool—The Little Black Book

Have a little black negotiation book to keep a log. Keep a separate page for each and every negotiation and keep track of:

1.) Who was there, names of parties involved, contact numbers

2.) The details of the item in question, i.e.: square footage of the building for purchase

3.) The price they wanted

4.) The price I wanted

5.) How much margin and room to move you have

6.) The renovation budgets or other improvement budgets

7.) The dates, what was said and what the final outcome of the interaction was

Predict the Future—Written Notes Win

Inside your black book of negotiation you should write out in advance the best case, realistic case, and worst case scenarios for your negotiation. If you have this done in advance you will be ahead of the other side that likely hasn't taken as much care in the preparation and outcome of the negotiation.

Have your contracts and paperwork ready before you begin the engagement and make it as easy as possible for the other side to agree to your proposal. If need be, have the paperwork filled out in advance.

Know all of your numbers and statistics such as what is this property worth today, how much does it need in repairs, and what is it worth after the repairs are done? How much profit will you make on this deal if you were to buy it at the right price? You would be surprised to know that the average person enters into a negotiation without proper facts and figures and usually cannot make an educated offer on the spot.

Before going in to meet the other side in live negotiation, make calls to your contacts for missing information if there is something you cannot find on your own.

In many ways, the battle is won and lost in the preparation phase, and if you fail to invest your time in this step, you will always enter the negotiation with a disadvantage. If you do well in a negotiation without proper preparation you are winning only because of luck. Truly successful people make their own luck by properly preparing.

Phase 1—The Collection Phase

"Know everything about the companies and people you are going to be negotiating with. Insist on getting the names of everyone participating in the negotiations. Leave no stone un- turned; find out as much as you can."

—Kevin O'Leary

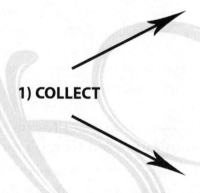

1) COLLECT

Once you have prepared adequately for the negotiation and be- gin to have first contact with the other side, you now enter the information collection phase. First contact could be a phone call, a meeting, or even a text or email, but I recommend making first contact over the phone or in person. Negotiation over text and email is never as effective as the phone or in person because the human element of body language and tone is left out of the equation, which accounts for 92 percent of communication.

Most novices fail at the collection phase because they fail to ask great questions and receive great answers. The collection phase is the beginning of the Three-C process and the beginning of the crescendo. As the negotiation expands, there will be more and more possibilities to make a deal as time goes on.

In the collection phase you want to give nothing and take everything when it comes to information. Avoid saying too much and avoid offering information; instead, let them do the talking. There is a saying in negotiation and selling that whoever is doing the talking is losing. Likewise, whoever is asking the questions is in control. If you do a good job of asking questions then you will have lots of ammunition when you move on the phase 2—the clutter phase, and they won't have much to work with when it comes to creating an offer and raising issues.

Speaking Their Language—Four Personality Styles

Understand that there are four types of negotiators out in the world, and each negotiator has a specific language that he speaks. If you approach the right negotiator with the right language you will be able to communicate. In contrast, if you have the wrong language for the wrong type of person, you will have major difficulties in striking a deal.

DISC—Dominance, Influence, Submission and Compliance

The DISC system was created by William Moulton Marston. In 1928, he published the book *Emotions of Normal People*. The history of DISC began with the elements of fire, earth, air, and water. The theory behind these four quadrants of personality style was originally written by Empodocles in 444 B.C.

Intuitively we know that there are four different types of people. If you watch any TV sitcom or any movie there are always these same four types of characters played over and over again. Whether it's the Simpsons (Homer, Marge, Lisa, Bart) or Seinfeld (Jerry, Elaine, George, Kramer) there are always four types of people that are balanced out by one another.

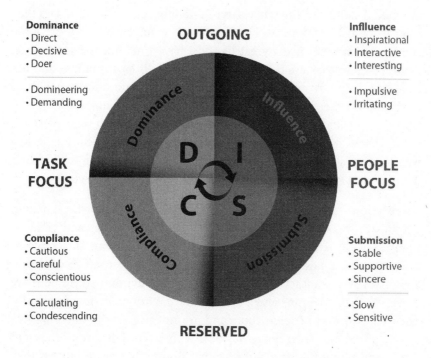

Dominance
- Direct
- Decisive
- Doer

- Domineering
- Demanding

OUTGOING

Influence
- Inspirational
- Interactive
- Interesting

- Impulsive
- Irritating

TASK FOCUS

PEOPLE FOCUS

Compliance
- Cautious
- Careful
- Conscientious

- Calculating
- Condescending

Submission
- Stable
- Supportive
- Sincere

- Slow
- Sensitive

RESERVED

Dominance—5% of the population. These are your fire, police, military, and business leaders. They are outgoing and task oriented; D is for direct. These people are results focused and want to get down to the bottom line immediately. They are task focused and seek to control their surroundings. They also believe that they are more powerful than their surroundings and believe that their surroundings are hostile. Dominance types are not interested in making friends; they are not interested in holding hands and singing "Kumbayah." They ask straight questions and want straight results. When you communicate with a D-type, deliver straight communication and give them results. If they were to choose a vehicle, they would likely choose a Mercedes and their favorite color would be black—the color of dominance.

Influence—35% of the population. High I-types are your natural sales people, advertising, marketing, public relations, tourism, retail, comedians, and on-stage performers. These people are outgoing and people oriented. I stands for Influence. I-types want to see and be seen, and they want to be friends, want to be liked, drink wine, have lunch, drive the convertible around, live a great lifestyle, have fun, and speak on stage. I-types believe they are more powerful than their surroundings and believe that their surroundings are friendly. When communicating with an I-type deliver them the sizzle, not the steak. They want to know how fast, fun, exciting, and cool looking the new idea is. They also want everyone to know how great it will look for them to make this new decision. If they were to choose a vehicle, they would choose the sexy convertible, and their favorite color would be red—a hot, flashy, look-at-me color.

Submission—35% of the population. S-types are your teachers, nurses, administrative, supporters, finance, HR, manufacturing, and generally nice people. They want stable, steady, supportive, and sincere communication. S-types also love guarantees, want to feel safe, secure, and legitimacy in a transaction. They perceive the environment to be more powerful than they are and perceive the environment to be friendly. They are reserved people-people and are not necessarily outgoing like the high I-types. When doing business with S-types they want the right thing, and they want to make sure that no one is getting hurt. If they were to choose a vehicle it would likely be a station wagon that could fit all of their friends and pets. Their favorite color of choice would be blue because it is calm and steady.

Compliance—25% of the population. C-types are engineers, accountants, attorneys, doctors, accountants, architects, and computer programmers. These people want statistics, facts and figures. They do not want to know that roughly half of the time the program is successful; they want to know that 48.34% of the time the program is successful. These people perceive the environment to be more powerful than them and that the environment is hostile. They are reserved, task oriented individuals who want to make decisions based on facts, figures, and statistics. When they make a decision they want to back it up with cold hard data and logic. If a compliance person were to choose a vehicle it would be a van or a truck because of the utility and usefulness and ability to haul things (even if they rarely haul goods), and their favorite color is irrelevant because it isn't statistically measurable.

Satisfying professions for the 4 personalities

D-Style 5% of the population

- Entrepreneurs
- Sales – Full Commission
- Sales Management
- Legal / Litigation
- Operations Management

I-Style 35% of the population

- Advertising / Marketing
- Public Relations
- Training
- Sales
- Hospitality / Tourism
- Retail – Sales

C-Style 25% of the population

- Accounting / Auditing
- Engineering
- Research and Development
- Quality Assurance / Safety
- Architecture
- Computer Programming

S-Style 35% of the population

- Teaching / Education
- Finance / Economics
- Human Resources
- Administration / Support Svcs
- Retail – Customer Service
- Manufacturing

When you meet the other side you must very quickly determine what type of person you are dealing with so that you can speak their language. Very quickly you can determine if they are outgoing or reserved and if they are people oriented or task oriented. From those two quick questions you can determine where they fit on the DISC axis.

People vs. Task based and Outgoing vs. Reserved?

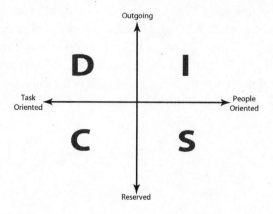

Collecting Information Effectively

You will always catch more flies with butter and honey than you will with poison: have a pleasing personality so that the other side likes you and will offer you information that they normally wouldn't give out.

Understand that negotiation is asymmetrical and what you want is likely not what they want. If you are buying a house, you might think price is the most important issue for both you and the vendor. In reality, both sides typically think that price is important but it is not the number one thing that will make or break the deal. You often don't want the same thing as the other side.

Find their hot buttons and find the irrational emotional things that they love

Many people will sell their homes dirty "as is" and take a discount of up to $20,000 to avoid cleaning the house. They will take a further discount of $5,000 or $20,000 if the house is full of junk because they don't want to pay someone $3,000 for trash removal. Maybe they don't have any cash on hand to pay someone the $3,000, or maybe they are just mentally lazy. Or maybe they don't want to do the work themselves. Or maybe the house is full of items that have emotional memories and they can't bear to sift through their past. In any case, walking away and paying a premium through a massive discount makes more irrational sense to them then the rational dollars and cents of cleaning out the house.

Another hot button may be that the buyers get to keep the furniture or they get to keep the TV. I often sell my homes with couches and TVs included because the buyer gets emotional and hot about one or two items. I once sold a home for a $7,000 premium because the buyer got emotional about the kitchen table and wanted to keep that specific kitchen table I had staged in the kitchen. In reality, the table was worth $250 but when bundled into the price of the house, it was a $7,000 premium. I've also sold TVs that are worth hundreds of dollars for thousands of dollars when they are bundled with the house because of the "gotta have it now" hot button.

What's your story? Digging for motivation

When I walk into a negotiation I will ask the other side, "What's your story?" When people start talking about their story they will typically give you too much information and their life story unabridged. By asking about their story you are trying to find out their true motivation and by doing this and they will usually give you two reasons why they are selling or buying. The first reason they will give you is usually a fabricated lie that sounds good to them and the second reason is the real reason that they don't want to tell you.

Their story will change over time as you continually ask what's their story over and over again.

In a "we buy houses" situation where the home seller is a hoarder, the seller hasn't called a realtor to sell the home because they are ashamed of the junk piled high to the ceiling in the home. They are ashamed of the dog pee and feces all over the carpet and the half-finished renovations. To be ashamed of the house is a hot button. There is major value to them in selling the home with ease, convenience, and discretion to help them save face with their neighbors and the neighborhood. The last thing these people want is for their neighbors, friends, and family to walk through the home and see the atrocity they have been living in.

To get the truth and avoid lies, you can ask the same question over and over again. Police, border guards, and authority figures ask the same questions over and over again to catch you in a lie. Are you here for business or pleasure? Are you here for business or pleasure? They will ask the same question at different times to catch you in a half truth or with a story that doesn't make sense. Break up the same question with other questions and come at them from different angles. Better questions create better answers.

The Formula For Creating Trust

In the collection phase it is most important that you find out the other side's motivation. Oftentimes when two parties are negotiating, it is hard to determine the real motivation of either side, because it's human nature to cover up our weaknesses. If we are motivated by weakness or a need, we will give a surface motivator rather than the real motivator. For example, you may be ninety days behind in your mortgage payments, and the sheriff may be coming to your home in the next seven days to evict you. You must sell your house, or you will lose it. Rather than telling the buyer that you are in foreclosure and will lose your home in seven days, you instead tell them that you just want to move into another part of town. Unfortunately, human nature dictates that human beings often seek to take advantage of one another and especially people who are vulnerable. Since we all understand this, when vulnerable, we will conceal or hide our weaknesses or real motivations.

To find the true motivation beneath a person's position you must establish trust. To establish trust and to trust another party you must have two things:

1.) Understand what motivates the other side.

    a. Their true motivation may be purposely hidden if it's a weakness.

    b. They may not know their true motivation, and you may have to find it.

    c. Their true motivation may be purposely concealed if they think it will hurt them when bargaining.

    d. They may tell you the real motivation up front to build trust.

2.) Have aligned self-interests.

    a. You may make an idealistic spiritual argument that humanity is altruistic and that self-interest doesn't matter. Studies show again and again that when resources are at stake, and especially if resources are scarce, human beings will act in their self-interest before the interest of others. Self-actualized people can think in terms of other people and the world is bigger than just themselves; however, the average person, who is not self-actualized, cannot see past himself. According to Ron Hubbard, there are eight dynamics or urges for survival, and each one builds on itself:

        i. The Self

ii. Your Mate or Family or Creativity

iii. The Group or Tribe

iv. The Species

v. Other Life Forms

vi. The Physical Universe

vii. The Spiritual Dynamic

viii. God or Infinity

When dealing with someone else, you can typically assume that they are acting in favor of themselves first and everything else is secondary.

b. You can only truly trust a man when you understand his interest.

c. You can trust an enemy better than a friend if you understand his self-interest and his motivation.

You may not find out what motivates the other side initially, for they may tell you something that is completely the opposite of their real needs. Likely, their true motivation will fall into one of the six basic human needs:

Six Basic Human Needs

According to Tony Robbins, every human being is motivated by the six basic human needs: certainty or comfort, uncertainty or variety, significance, love and connection, growth and contribution. These basic human needs are defined as follows:

1.) **Certainty or comfort**—The need for security, safety, being in control, basic comfort, avoidance of pain and stress, to create pleasure. This need is ultimately our survival mechanism and our risk tolerance. A person with a low risk tolerance will have a high need for certainty. Most people are motivated by certainty as one of their strongest motivators.

2.) **Uncertainty or variety**—Too much certainty breeds boredom so to balance out the need for certainty is the need for variety. Have you ever started a new diet and then gotten bored and eaten something you weren't supposed to eat? That is your need for variety coming into play. The surprises you want in life are called surprises, and they are fun. The surprises you don't want are called problems. Whether your surprises are wanted or not, they are a major need for every human being.

3.) **Significance**—The need to be important, special, unique or needed. To fill our need for significance, we may go out and make a million dollars, get a TV show, complain to others about our problems, collect academic degrees, cheat on our spouse, get tattoos and piercings, build a huge social media following, or becoming more spiritual than others (or at least pretending to be). Most people are motivated by significance and comfort, and when those two needs are your top two of the six, you will be stuck at the same spot in life until you reprioritize your needs. Spending a lot of money can fill your need for significance along with spending as little money as possible; both are functions of the same need. Steve Wynn capitalized on people's need for significance when he built "the best" casino hotels in Las Vegas. Anyone with a large need for significance will always pay a premium for the best, and even if they won't pay, they will always want the best.

4.) **Love and connection**—Love is the oxygen of life, and when we are in love we feel completely alive. If we lose our love, we will settle on connection. Connection is built through intimacy, prayer, or walking in nature, and if all else fails, you can get a dog.

Needs 1–4 are called the needs of the personality. Needs 5 and 6 are the needs of the spirit. A person may go through life only appealing to needs 1–4. To be truly fulfilled in life, we must move past the first four human needs: certainty, uncertainty, significance, and love and connection, which occur inside of ourselves and onto the spiritual needs of growth and contribution which allow us to bring value to people outside of ourselves.

5.) **Growth**—In life, you are either growing or dying. You are either getting better or getting worse. In business, your business either grows or it shrinks; it is impossible to stay the same in life or business. Growth is a spiritual need and one that is required for real fulfilment. The reason to grow typically comes from the belief that we have something of value to give.

6.) **Contribution**—The secret to a fulfilled life is to give. There are only two ways to emit light: (1) be the candle or (2) be the mirror reflecting the candle. Either way, we must give to truly live. Sharing enhances the human experience and the emotions felt when getting are the same brain mechanisms that are triggered when giving. In life, it's not what you get that will make you happy, but ultimately who you will become in the process of living. Ask yourself: When you die, who will show up to your funeral? If you live a life of service and contribution, there will be many people showing up to your funeral. However, if everything you do is self-serving, you may be buried alone.

When to Move from Phase 1 Collecting to Phase 2 Cluttering?

Stay in the collection phase as long as possible. Eighty percent of your time needs to be spent collecting information and only when you are fully confident that you have collected enough information to make a smart offer to you move on the phase 2—the clutter phase.

Phase 2—The Clutter Phase: Raise Issues and Make an Offer

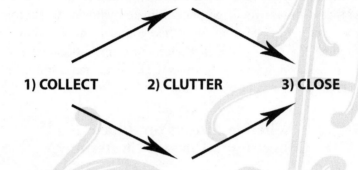

1) COLLECT   **2) CLUTTER**   **3) CLOSE**

Deception is power. Power these days is not about the biggest guns or the biggest muscles. Instead it is the ability to conceal your position and potentially deceive the other side.

The clutter phase is where the bulge in the crescendo begins to appear. The bulge means that the amount of possibilities in the negotiation is hitting its critical mass, and anything can happen in the middle of a negotiation.

Buyers are liars, and sellers are liars. The middle of the negotiation, the clutter, is the fun part of the negotiation. No one really knows what is true and what is a fabrication, and each and every claim must be tested for validity. Both sides are lying to each other not because it's wrong or they are malicious; instead it is human nature to conceal their position and try to get the most out of the negotiation. It's not wrong or right, and we aren't making an ethical judgement on the things that people say when negotiating. The fact that remains true about negotiating is that people do not like to reveal their positions for fear of being taken advantage of by the other side. Much like retail buyers who walk into a store and when approached by a salesperson, they reply that they are "just looking" even though they are serious buyers. They don't want to be sold, but they do want to buy.

The clutter phase, phase 2, is where issues are raised, and clutter is created. Most people are afraid to clutter; they are afraid of raising issues and causing conflict. There is absolutely nothing wrong with raising issues in a negotiation, and in fact, this is where the negotiating really starts: when one side starts raising issues.

Understand that what they want is not necessarily what you want, and to measure all of the small points of the negotiation, we can track what both sides want by using a negotiation T-chart.

MY COUNTER

US	THEM

Negotiation T-Chart

When negotiating we create clutter by raising issues. The other side does not know which issues are real and which are decoys. When negotiating, the person who creates more clutter and raises more issues usually ends up with a better deal because they have more items to trade later on.

Sample Negotiation #1— We Buy Houses Motivated Seller

In this scenario we have "us," a buyer of distressed homes, and a "them," a distressed seller that wants a high price for their house, no hassle, no mess, and no headache.

Outlined below is a T-chart of wants for both sides lined up point for point.

WANTS

US	THEM
• Low Price	• High Price
• Slow Possession	• Fast Possession
• Fresh Coat of Paint	• Sell As-Is
• Vendor Take Back	• All Cash
• Vendor to Clean Yard	• No Hassle
• Vendor to Remove Trash	• No Mess
• Vendor to Fix Garage	• No Reno's
• Conditional Offer	• Guaranteed Close
• Ask for Survey	• No Headache
• Small Deposit	• Big Deposit

The side with the most items to trade usually wins. Normal people do not usually have a whole stack of items that they are demanding. Most people have one or two items that they really want in any given negotiation. If you walk into a negotiation demanding twelve items and they only want one or two items, you will dominate the other side when you begin to trade items by sheer numbers. In one or two trades you will have most of what you want, and the other side will have no more ammunition.

As the negotiation progresses, items will get traded, challenged, and phased out when you enter phase 3. Until you challenge an item or a demand, you don't know if that item is real or a decoy. Challenge everything to find resistance and the real values of the other side.

Stacking up items, demands, and issues on your list of wants is a great way to come in with a high value offer. When making an offer, typically both sides are blind and can only rely on the information they collected during the collection phase.

In this sample negotiation when the items began to get challenged and traded, it became apparent that price was not the most important thing for the motivated seller.

THE OFFER

US	THEM
• Low Price	• ~~High Price~~
• ~~Slow Possession~~	• Fast Possession
• ~~Fresh Coat of Paint~~	• Sell As-Is
• ~~Vendor Take Back~~	• All Cash
• ~~Vendor to Clean Yard~~	• No Hassle
• ~~Vendor to Remove Trash~~	• No Mess
• ~~Vendor to Fix Garage~~	• No Reno's
• ~~Conditional Offer~~	• Guaranteed Close
• ~~Ask for Survey~~	• No Headache
• ~~Small Deposit~~	• Big Deposit

In this example we closed the gap on price by trading the items we didn't want for concessions on the price. As it turns out, convenience, speed, and a guaranteed close were very important to this motivated seller and they are winning on nine to ten items that are important to them, mostly terms for quick, fast, and easy sale. We are winning on the one item that was important to us, which was price. The other side doesn't value price as much because they want a "no hassle and no mess" transaction, and that is why this negotiation works.

Needs versus Wants

On the other side's value stack they have a list of items, some are needs and some are wants. Wants and needs are two very different things. Notice that if you ask the other side what they want, they will give you a very different answer then if you ask what they need later on.

Example: What do you want x3?

You ask: "What do you want for the house, John?" He'll say "$100,000."

Later in the negotiation you ask again as you raise issues and his aspiration level drops: "What do you want for the house, John?" "He'll say $90,000."

Later in the negotiation you ask again as you raise more issues and his aspiration level drops more "What do you actually want for the house, John?" "He'll say $85,000."

Later in the negotiation you ask with all of the issues on the table not about his wants but instead about his needs: "But what do you need for the house, John?" "He'll say "$76,000."

Start with wants when the other side's aspiration levels are high and then change to needs as their aspirations drop while you raise issue after issue.

The Rate Of Concession And Who Will Win The Negotiation?

There is a term used when studying negotiation called the "rate of concession." Typically in a negotiation, the person who makes the first large concession is the person who will "lose" the negotiation and walk away with a worse deal than the other side. When negotiating, monitor your rate of concession and how fast and how big you give things away. Typically a big concession that happens fast will result in demands for more large concessions. In contrast, small concessions given slowly will result in a better position for you over all. Humans by nature subconsciously or consciously pay attention to the rate of concession and if they watch you drop the price too fast they will either think (1) that your offer has no value, or (2) there must be something wrong with your offer. Either way, let the other side give the first major concession and avoid giving large concessions quickly.

Phase 3—The Close—Trading Points And Getting What You Want

After we have made an offer and raised issues in Phase 2, the clutter phase, we move onto Phase 3—The Close and trading points to get what you want.

Once all of the issues are on the table, we are going to challenge their issues for validity, and when we make trades, we are going to ask for everything and charge for every single concession. When you make concessions, make them small and always ask for something in return to maintain your value. Statistically, the side that makes the first big concession usually has to make bigger concessions later on and comes out with a worse deal than the side that holds their value.

Every single issue that you raise, term, condition or piece of clutter such as: "no hassle no mess," "Sell without a survey," "Sell without a fresh coat of paint" is worth a real dollar amount to someone and every piece that you give away has to be paid for by the other side in either real dollars or in concessions of equal or greater value.

When you charge for concessions and capture the points that you are giving away, you maintain the value of your value stack, and the longer you can hold your value high, the better your position to win.

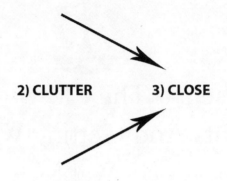

2) CLUTTER   **3) CLOSE**

THE TRADES

US	THEM
• ~~Low Price~~	• ~~High Price~~
• ~~Slow Possession~~	• Fast Possession
• ~~Fresh Coat of Paint~~	• Sell As-Is
• ~~Vendor Take Back~~	• All Cash
• Vendor to Clean Yard	• ~~No Hassle~~
• Vendor to Remove Trash	• ~~No Mess~~
• Vendor to Fix Garage	• ~~No Reno's~~
• ~~Conditional Offer~~	• Guaranteed Close
• ~~Ask for Survey~~	• ~~No Headache~~
• Small Deposit	• ~~Big Deposit~~
• New Low Price	

Example: We Buy Houses Motivated Seller #2

In this scenario we have another motivated home seller who wanted to sell fast but wanted more money than the previous home seller. So instead of taking a fire-sale price, this vendor was willing to (1) clean the yard, (2) remove the trash from the property, and (3) fix the garage, and in return for some of those services, we, the home buyer, were willing to pay a slightly higher, but still low price for the house.

In this example we made trades for the things that we wanted, gave away the low value items we did not want as much, and took the high value items that we needed such at a slightly higher low price in exchange for all of the work the vendor was willing to do.

Every time the other side wants to change the deal or make an amendment, charge them by taking something in return. Keep your value high and equal to your opening position of extreme value. Every time they want something, you need to take something somewhere else.

Get what you want, give them what they need, and make them pay for what they truly want.

WANTS

US	THEM
• Low Price	• High Price
• Slow Possession	• Fast Possession
• Fresh Coat of Paint	• Sell As-Is
• Vendor Take Back	• All Cash
• Vendor to Clean Yard	• No Hassle
• Vendor to Remove Trash	• No Mess
• Vendor to Fix Garage	• No Reno's
• Conditional Offer	• Guaranteed Close
• Ask for Survey	• No Headache
• Small Deposit	• Big Deposit

Example: We Are A Retail Home Seller, Brand New Flip House

In this example we are the seller of a brand new flip house that we have just renovated. In fact, it could be the renovated and polished version of the "we buy houses" example above. In this example we want to sell "as is" full price, no hassle, no mess, with a big deposit, no appliances, and no TV included. The other side wants a $10,000 discount (just because), appliances included and a list of small items including a survey, cleaned yard, fixed garage, dad inspection, all appliances, and even the TV!

In this negotiation we challenge all of the buyer's points and through challenging them we find that the fake, less important points fall away as we begin to challenge their position.

105

MY COUNTER

US	THEM
• ~~Full Price~~	• ~~10k Discount~~
• ~~Fast Possession~~	• ~~Slow Possession~~
• Sell As Is	• ~~Doors Fixed~~
• ~~All Cash~~	• Financing
• No Hassle	• ~~Vendor to clean yard~~
• No Mess	• ~~Vendor to remove trash~~
• No Reno's	• ~~Vendor to fix garage~~
• ~~Guaranteed Close~~	• Dad Inspection
• No Headache	• ~~Ask for survey~~
• Big Deposit	• ~~Small Deposit~~
• No Appliances	• All Appliances
• No TV	• ~~TV~~
• Halfway Price	
• Halfway Possession	

Through smart trading, fake points fall away, and we are left with the core issues. In this example, the points that were highest value to the first time home buyers were:

1.) Financing because they have never bought a home before and are scared that they will not qualify for financing.

2.) The Dad inspection because it's emotional; they are young buyers who want father's approval.

3.) Appliances included because they have no more money after paying their down payment. They don't want to go into consumer debt to pay for appliances so they would rather have the brand new ones included with their house purchase and rolled into their mortgage.

The first time home buyers came in with twelve items of clutter and through trading with us, ended up with three pieces that they actually wanted.

On our side, we came out with a higher price because we traded well and in this example, the appliances were so valuable that they gave away the rest of their positions to claim the positions that were most valuable.

Two Main Styles Of Negotiation

"The best move you can make in negotiation is to think of an incentive the other person hasn't even thought of—and then meet it."

—Eli Broad

When negotiating there are two main styles of negotiation that you will see in the field: competitive or adversarial style and co-operative style negotiation.

Competitive or Adversarial Style: Negotiation typically takes place where there are a fixed number of limited resources. For example, two parties may be negotiating their share of a large apple pie. They are competing to see who can get the biggest slice of pie and let the other side walk away with the smaller slice of pie. There is only a fixed amount of pie with a fixed amount of apples in it and a fixed amount of crumbs. There is no potential for creating more pie or making the deal bigger. The resources are scarce, and both sides are adversarial. When one side wins a bigger slice of the pie, the other side gets a smaller slice. This is also known as win-lose negotiation where one side wins, and the other side loses. Many industries and most people operate from a competitive or adversarial style of negotiation. This is a scarcity-driven style that can create harsh feelings, aggression, fighting, or even enemies between negotiators.

Cooperative Negotiation: The opposite style of competitive negotiation or adversarial negotiation is cooperative negotiation, sometimes called "both win" negotiation. In cooperative negotiation, rather than competing for bigger slices of a single apple pie, the two parties find a way to bring in a second pie so there is more to share. This method focuses on building greater value and increasing the amount of pie that would be divided. While adversarial or competitive negotiation focuses on competing for a scarce amount of pie, cooperative negotiation focuses on creating an abundance of pie to be shared by all. In business, your income is directly correlated to your ability create more pie and cooperate. Create massive value and share rather than fighting for a small bargain.

Ten Ways To Fail Using The Three-C System

Although the Three-C negotiation system is simple, it isn't easy in practice. Here are some of the pitfalls that less experienced negotiators succumb to when making early attempts to negotiate.

1.) **They skip preparation**—Preparation begins before we make contact with the other side. For many people preparation is on the "should have done it" list but is never really a major priority. Do the research and gain a better position immediately!

2.) **They rush the collection period**—Asking hard questions can be uncomfortable and we all want to rush through it as quick as possible. Spend 80 percent of your time collecting information and asking questions so that you can make an educated offer with enough points to trade.

3.) **No questions or the wrong questions**—By asking no questions or the wrong questions, novice negotiators often miss capturing the fundamental motivation on the other side and thus can't make an offer that makes sense.

4.) **They forget to clutter**—Many novice negotiators make the negotiation all about price and forget to build value by raising ten to twelve pieces of clutter so that they can trade on terms as well.

5.) **They build zero value in their offer**—Always build an offer of greater value. Sell your offer and why it is best for the other side, whether you are offering the best price or not.

6.) **They trade poorly**—Trading points can be complex, and if you don't have clearly written goals you can make bad trades or forget about what you are trading for.

7.) **They speak to the wrong style of DISC**—Speaking to the wrong style of the DISC is a quick way to deadlock a negotiation and get nowhere. If you aren't speaking the language of the other side, you will have a low chance of coming out ahead.

8.) **Try to close to early**—Many novice negotiators skip the entire process and try to close too early without proper questioning or without raising clutter. Don't try to close in on main issues until you are convinced that you have followed the Three-C process thoroughly and have made all of the necessary trades.

9.) **Try to negotiate too fast**—Slow down! The longer the negotiation, the higher the level of commitment on all parties. When the commitment is high, all parties are more invested in bringing the negotiation to a favorable conclusion. When necessary, do anything you can to increase the commitment of the other side.

10.) **They give the first big concession**—Studies show that the negotiator who gives the first big concession typically ends up with a worse position than he had hoped for. Avoid giving the first big concession.

Part IV:
30 Laws Of Human Nature

*With gambits, moves and countermoves
to gain your advantage*

Thirty Laws
Of Human Nature

And Thirty Practical Gambits
To Gain An Advantage

"Negotiating means getting the best of your opponent."

—MARVIN GAYE

Every great general, leader, businessman, and artist in history has understood one thing well: human nature. As a whole, humanity is just self-destructive enough to keep ourselves from reaching our true potential and just self preserving enough to avoid wiping ourselves out. Since the days of Shakespeare and back to the Romans and the Greeks, technology has changed, social movements have come and gone, empires have risen and fallen, but the one thing that remains the same is human nature.

Regardless of technology, regardless of social movements, regardless of which empire is in power today or tomorrow, human nature remains unchanging. The writings of the Greek philosophers, Roman emperors, and Shakespearean plays are still as relevant today as they were hundreds or even thousands of years ago. Our brains are more complex than the most powerful super computer today, but we are still primitive creatures driven by self-interest and ruled by emotion.

If you want to be powerful, if you want to be influential, if you want to be effective at getting what you want in life and in business, you must become a student of human nature.

In this section I have outlined laws of human nature that are timeless whether you are in ancient Greece or in modern-day America. Each law of human nature has been carefully selected as an observation of the way people are, and then I have provided a gambit, or a move to exploit this law of human nature. I have also provided a counter-move in case you find someone else exploiting this law against you.

Gambit is a chess term derived from the italian word *gambetto*, which means "to trip." In chess, a gambit is used to "trip up" an opponent and gain a time advantage or positioning advantage. In chess, gambits are offered to the other side and are either "accepted" or "declined" in the same way that a hunter would offer a trap to a fox.

Law #1: Exploit the Need to Reinforce Previous Decisions

Practical Gambit: The Nibble

"Everything is negotiable. Whether or not the negotiation is easy is another thing."

—CARRIE FISHER

Human beings are pattern-recognizing machines. We seek to find patterns in nature, in mathematics, and in social structure, and when we find a favorable pattern, we want it to continue. Patterns are like habits, and even if a pattern is a negative one, like addictions or abuse, we seem to rationalize our future actions to fit in with our past actions. In some ways, human beings have a need to reinforce previous decisions whether they make sense or not and keep the patterns either to our benefit or our detriment.

A young woman and her mother are cooking a ham for the holidays, and her mother cuts off both ends of the ham and places it in the pot. The young woman asks her mother, "Why did we cut the ends off the ham?"

Her mother replies, "I don't know; let me ask my mother."

So the mother calls her mother and asks, "Mother, why do we cut the ends off the ham before we put it in the pot?"

Her mother replies, "I don't know; let me call my mother and find out."

So they call the mother of the mother's mother and ask, "Why do we cut the ends off the ham?" Great-grandma says, "Because my pot was too small and the ham wouldn't fit."

In this story, the women are cutting the ends off of the ham to reinforce the previous decisions that were made about cutting the ends off the ham. They are reinforcing the status quo and are merely continuing the pattern of cutting off the ends of the ham whether it makes sense or not.

When negotiating you can exploit the other side's need to reinforce previous decisions. "This is the deal I have been offered in the past," "Previous pricing has been the same," "Typically our customers pay ...," and "Company policy" are some phrases that reinforce previous decisions and can keep previous patterns going on indefinitely. If that is the way things have always been, then that is how they should remain is a common attitude among average people because the average man lacks vision and cannot see things any other way.

Practical Gambit: The Nibble

When negotiating, take advantage of the other side's desire to reinforce their previous decisions.

Move—After the major decisions have been established, at the point of agreement, after shaking hands or signing paperwork, ask for something more. The other side, wanting to reinforce their previous decision of agreement, will find it hard to say no to your "nibble" because they have just made a big decision that they need to reinforce.

Example: After agreeing to a purchase price on a house you are purchasing you can say as you shake hands, "by the way, could you haul away all the junk in the back yard and fix the broken window?" The need to reinforce the previous decision to sell the home and agree on price is so strong that the broken window and cleaning up the trash seem immaterial relative to the larger decision that has just been made.

When negotiating with Mexican street vendors I made an offer on a beautiful horse statue supposidly carved from fish bones. The street vendor wanted $200 American dollars for the statue, and I was only prepared to pay $50 for the statue. After many offers, walk aways, and renegotiations over several hours, I approached the vendor as he was taking down his stand at nearly midnight. He was wrapping up his statues and getting ready to go home, and finally I offered him my $50 again for the horse statue. Since it was the end of the night and he was packing up, he sold me the horse for $50, but once we had agreed and I pulled out my wallet, his amigo approached me and said, "Señor, we have been here all night and our boss will not be happy that we got you such a good price on such a beautiful statue, could you give us a little tip of two American dollars?" As this Mexican aquaintance was asking me for a two dollar tip, the street vendor was wrapping up my statue carefully and I was feeling good about my decision to get the horse at such a price that I pulled out my wallet and gave his associate $2 to reinforce my previous decision. After I gave the Mexican side kick $2, he continued, "and Señor, surely we are thirsty after being here in the heat all night, could you go to your room and get us each a Coca-Cola? We will give you the statue to take to your room, you don't even have to pay us now. We will just take your room number and we trust you. Please just bring us two Coca-Cola's." I couldn't believe their tact. These Mexican negotiators were going to let me take the horse statue back to my room, no money down, to get them two free Cokes that they want thrown into the deal. Then I'm going to pay them an extra $2 tip to walk all the way across the resort at midnight so they can nibble two Cokes. In the moment of victory in the negotiation, how could I refuse? I took the horse statue back to my room, carefully wrapped in newspaper, and I returned to give my vendors two Coca-Colas, a $2 tip (one dollar for each negotiator), and the $50 cash that they needed for the horse. The Mexicans were masters of nibbling, and they knew that I would never refuse a relatively small request that could jeopordize my relatively larger buying decision that I made earlier.

Counter Move—No one wants to feel like a cheapskate and if you catch someone nibbling you for extra concessions simply say "Oh c'mon, you already got a great deal! Don't be so cheap!"

In Mexico the Mexican street negotiators will laugh at you with a smile when you try to nibble and say "why you gotta be so Mexican?!"

Law #2: Avoid Absorbing Other People's Problems

Practical Gambit: Hot Potato or "Not My Problem"

"Avoid the Unhappy and the Unlucky"

—ROBERT GREENE, 48 LAWS OF POWER

"You have to persuade yourself that you absolutely don't care what happens. If you don't care, you've won. I absolutely promise you, in every serious negotiation, the man or woman who doesn't care is going to win."

— FELIX DENNIS

Powerful negotiators know that unhappiness and unluckiness are infectious diseases that need to be avoided at all costs. There are certain types of negotiators that will try to pass their problems off onto you. Some examples of other people trying to pass their problems to you might be: "We can only afford a car $30,000 or less," "Our financing will only support a house up to $150,000," "our budget for this renovation is only $10,000." What the other side is expecting is that you absorb their problem or their constraint and work within the restrictions they are giving you. They want to make their problem your problem, and since human beings sincerely want to help one another, novice negotiators will absorb the problem and try to sort it out for the other side.

Practical Gambit: Hot Potato or "Not My Problem"

Move—Someone is trying to pass their problem onto you, known as "passing you the hot potato." For example: "We can only afford $150,000 for our house purchase because the bank is limiting our credit."

Counter Move—Test the other side's problem for validity: "Can you show me written proof from the bank that $150,000 is the maximum that you can pay?" or simply use the line: "That's not my problem, tell your clients to find more money!" The phrase "not my problem" is a very powerful way of separating the pity from reality. Another counter that you can use on the "hot potato" is to pass the hot potato right back to the other side. For example: a contractor gives you an unfavorable quote on a renovation you need to do at $40,000 for a house renovation. Your budget is only $30,000, and they are $10,000 over budget. You can simply call the contractor back and say, "I love your quote. I think I want to work with you; we only have one problem: I need the same work done for $30,000 and not a penny more. Take some time to go over your numbers, find some efficiencies, and call me back when you can make it fit into $30,000. Thank you." More often than not when you pass the hot potato back to the other side and give them a specific box to fit into, they will do their best to fit into your proposal. Make your problems their problems and avoid absorbing other people's problems.

Absorbing other people's problems will wear you down and waste your energy. Don't allow other people to waste your energy.

Law #3: Displaced Authority Is Real Authority

Practical Gambit—Displace Authority

"Follow an expert."

—Virgil

Human beings have a need to look to others for authority. The word *authority* has the word "author" inside of it, and the "author" is the person who wrote the rules. You must understand that the person who wrote the rules is no different than you. When negotiating we lose our bargaining power when we are positioned as the decision makers with the ability to make concessions. Parents with small children will know that their little boy or girl is a fierce negotiator who does not take "no" for an answer and will adopt the routine of "ask your mom" or "ask your dad." Displacing authority makes the authority appear to be real. Mom may be the decision maker, but she will defer authority onto dad or vice versa. The same thing happens on car lots every day. The salesperson will make a proposal to a customer with a price and terms for a certain automobile. The customer will ask for a discount or some type of concession and then the salesman will have to "check with the manager," which means leaving the line of sight and checking with his higher power. The common excuse heard in direct sales "let me check with my wife" is a reflex that most men will utter to get out of a sales presentation. In reality, the man of the house is likely the final decision maker, but he will displace authority to send away an undetermined saleperson.

Move—Always displace your authority onto someone else. This may feel bad for your ego, but it's good for business. Even if you are the decision maker, get in the habit of always answering to someone else. You may own the company but you must still answer to "a committee of investors." Instead of positioning yourself as the "president," call yourself the "vice president" with an undetermined president. When displacing authority, the more vague, the better. A comittee of people or a group of partners is much more difficult to track down or assemble into a decision-making group. When the authority you answer to is vague, you have power.

Example—Say: I like your offer, but I have to run it by my committee. (a committee is an undefined group of people—keep it vague.) The entire real estate industry runs on the principle of deferred authority. Studies have shown that sellers of property make much worse deals with buyers than had they hired an agent to act on their behalf. This is the main reason why most property sellers choose to sell through a professional real estate agent instead of selling the property themselves. The ability for the agent to defer authority and be detached from the negotiation creates power for the seller and disarms a savvy buyer who would do much better by negotiating direct. A seller will do so much better through this method that it justifies the 3–7% fee that the real estate salesperson will charge for negotiating and deferring authority.

Countermove—To disarm the deferral of authoirty, get commitment that they are the decision maker up front and refuse to deal with them unless they have the decision maker. For example, a real estate salesperson may say: "If we find the right property today would there be any reason to not go ahead?" In the direct sales industry, there is often a policy: "no one leggers." A one legger refers to a sales presentation made for just a husband or just a wife. Salespeople in the direct sales industry know that if they make a presentation without both decision makers in the room it will ruin the chances of making a sale. In direct sales they will often offer incentives to get both decision makers in the room such as show tickets, vacations, free food, and so on. If both decision makers don't show up, the presentation isn't made. Don't waste your time dealing with people who are not decision makers.

Three-Step Counter to Displaced Authority

Perhaps you get stuck making an offer to someone who does not have all of the decision making power. Here is the countermove:

> Step 1) Appeal to their ego. Example: "Mr. Vice president, I know you do great work for your organization, and I know you aren't the final decision maker, but you certainly are capable of making the right decision."
>
> Step 2) Get their commitment.
>
> > "And you will recommend my proposal, won't you?"
>
> Step 3) "Subject to" close
>
> > "Wonderful; let's draw up a contract subject to the president's approval and then we could both save ourselves some time by getting all of the details worked out now."

By following that three-step counter to displaced authority, you will quickly find out if the agent you are dealing with is on board with your proposal or not. If the agent is not on board, you might need to approach the negotiation from another angle.

Law #4: Have the Easy Conversations First and the Hard Conversations Last

Practical Gambit: Breaking an Impasse— The "Set-Aside Technique"

"It is easier to resist at the beginning than at the end."

—LEONARDO DA VINCI

"Your success in life is directly proportionate to your ability to have hard conversations."

—STEFAN AARNIO

All human relationships are based on one thing—agreement. Without agreement, we have no relationships. Think of any person you enjoy being around—perhaps a spouse, family member, friend, or business partner. Anyone you enjoy being around and transacting with is a person you share a high level of agreement with. To be successful when negotiating with someone who may or may not like us, we need to build momentum and quickly build a relationship based on agreement. Instead of going "head to head" on the big issues like price or the bottom line when negotiating, you can take the back-door approach and create agreement on all the small details first to create momentum, agreement, and rapport. Some smaller items you can create agreement on would be payment terms, deposits, delivery date, color, size, duration of contract, guarantees, condition of product, promptness of service, warranties, delivery charges, upgrades, conditions, and so on. Most people forget about all of the other factors when negotiating and make everything all about price or the bottom line. In many cases the price is important, but the terms are just as important!

Move—"Breaking an impasse": An impasse is where the other side is forceful and won't budge on one item.

Example: You may be trying to purchase a residential house for a discount, and the seller says: "No matter what, I need to get $100,000 for this property; it's my bottom line"

Countermove—You say, "Okay, no problem. Let's set aside the issue of price for a moment and talk about the closing date; would you be okay with October 1st?"

By settling on the small issues first and creating commitment you are increasing your odds and chances on dealing with the big issues at the end. People are less likely to walk away from something that they are invested in, and you are creating commitment by creating agreement. Settle on all the small issues first, increase commitment, and then when you have built up momentum, start settling the bigger issues. Oftentimes people are thinking one dimensionally when they approach a negotiation. By settling the small issues first, you can build value in your offer by showing value in the terms as well as the price.

Law #5: Create The Illusion Of Fairness

Practical Gambit—Solving A Deadlock—The Neutral Third Party

A fundamentalist can't bring himself or herself to negotiate with people who disagree with them because the negotiating process itself is an indication of implied equality.

—Jimmy Carter

We live in a world today that teaches children from kindergarten and onward that "life is fair." We preach fairness, equality, democracy, and "every vote counts." Gone are the days of kings and queens, lords, castes, and classes. People want to believe that they are equal to others and that life is fair. In reality, life is not fair and neither is business. There is always someone who has an advantage, someone who has more, someone who is taller or better looking, or someone who has a nicer smile. There is no such thing as equal, and equality can never be achieved. Countries have attempted to create equality through communism in the past to make every man equal, but the systems of forced equality do not work.

"Socialism is a philosophy of failure, the creed of ignorance, and the gospel of envy, its inherent virtue is the equal sharing of misery."

— Winston Churchill

Nonetheless, people have a desire to feel as though they have a fair chance. They want to feel like everyone can succeed and that the game they are playing is not rigged against them. As rigged as the game may be, we want to think that the game is fair.

We want to believe that any man or woman in America can run for president, but in reality, presidency is reserved for an elite few. The cost of a presidential campaign will run in the millions and sometimes even in the billions by the time the smoke clears. While the average man in theory could become president, in reality, it is nearly impossible.

There is a philosophy in the Western world that if you go to school, get a job, and work hard, you will succeed. Life is fair; hard work is rewarded. In reality, although hard work and success are correlated, life is not fair. A baseball star in the major league baseball league will make $2,000,000 a year to hit a baseball very well with a bat, while a school teacher will get paid $30,000 to shape the lives of children. Who has a bigger impact and who is worth more in real value? The answer is that life is not fair, and it doesn't really matter who is worth more. Although life is not fair, people need to feel that there is an illusion of fairness.

We need to feel like anyone can run for president so we don't revolt againsyt the system. We need to feel like anyone can become a baseball star if they work really hard. We need to feel like anyone can make it regardless of advantages or disadvantages to keep people from lashing out against other people. When negotiating, power is rarely evenly distributed. One party usually has power over the other or some form of leverage, and the other party may have less power. However, even though there is a disparity in power, the powerful thing to do for the person with more power is to create an illusion of fairness and a feeling that the playing field is level. People want to work with people like them. They want to do deals and transact with others who are similar and equal to them. One side may have more power, but using power against others directly is in bad taste, and it's much better to create an illusion of fairness and let the other side strike a deal rather than forcing power over them.

If you have more power and fail to create an illusion of fairness when negotiating, the other side may realize that they indeed have no power at all and no power becomes its own form of dangerous power. There is nothing more dangerous than a man with nothing to lose or a man with everything to gain. If you have a power disparity, the best thing to do is to make the man with less power feel equal and be fair with him. Otherwise, should he discover the power of "no power," you may create a massive shift in power that could put you out of power. An example of no power would be a teenager who refuses to do his homework: what can the parents really do? Throw him out of the house? He would have no where to live! Take away his dinner? Then he will have to steal or run away! Charge him a fine? He has no money! That will only create more problems for the father and mother, and ultimately, by forcing power on him, they may create a criminal in the process. They would be much better off to create an illusion of fairness with him and share an open dialogue with both sides winning in the process. Another example of "no power" would be the prison inmate who has had all privelidges stripped of him and is now in solitary confinement throwing his own feces at the prison guards. What are the gaurds going to do? The man has absolutely nothing, and they can't do anything legal to make him stop. It's best to create an illusion of fairness with him and give him something to lose. Another example of "no power" with nothing to lose are small rogue terrorist groups that may get their hands on nuclear weapons. These small groups have nothing to lose by setting off a nuclear explosion and sowing terror in major cities and countries. Large countries like the United States are terrified of enemies with "no power" because although they spend as much money on military defense as the rest of the world combined, no amount of aircraft carriers, F-22 fighter planes, ballistic missiles, or tanks can save you from a man with "no power." The only way to disarm a man with no power is to creating an illusion of fairness and give the man choice and something to win and something to lose.

Practical Gambit—Solving A Deadlock—The Neutral Third Party

Often in negotiating, two parties will reach a disparity in price or terms and the negotiation enters a deadlock. According to google, the definition of a deadlock is:

dead·lock ded läk/

1. a situation, typically one involving opposing parties, in which no progress can be made. "an attempt to break the deadlock"

2. British term for deadbolt.

3. cause (a situation or opposing parties) to come to a point where no progress can be made because of fundamental disagreement. "the jurors were deadlocked on six charges"

It does not take a genius to put a negotiation into a deadlock, but it certainly takes a genius to get a negotiation out of a deadlock and back into agreement.

Move—Your negotiation is frozen in a deadlock: both sides disagree on a major point, and neither side wants to give in. Since there is no agreement, any chance of a deal are rapidly diminishing.

Example: You are purchasing a distressed residential home to buy, fix, and sell for profit. The seller is an investor who purchased a run-down house and has subdivided the side yard into an extra lot. The lot has been sold for profit, and the investor now wants to sell you the run-down house for an agreeable price. You have agreed to a price, a closing date, a deposit, and so on. But the deal does not close because the city wants one wall of the house fireproofed before the subdivision can go through. You have your financing lined up, your investors lined up, your constuction team lined up, but the deal closing date keeps getting pushed further and further into the future. Finally, you meet the seller to discuss the deal to see if this deal will ever close. The new issue of the fireproofed wall comes up, and you believe the seller should pay for the fireproofing while they believe that you, the buyer, should pay for the fireproofing. You know that the seller cannot sell the home until the fireproofing is done for their land deal to go through, so you have all of the power. Finally, the seller agrees to pay for the fireproofing of the wall, but how much? The negotiation is deadlocked over how much to pay for the fireproofed wall. You believe the wall will cost $10,000 so you want $10,000 off of the purchase price and the seller believes that the fireproofing will only cost $2,000. You are $8,000 apart. To break the deadlock you call in a "neutral third party." You open the phone book and call the three contractors with the biggest, most expensive ads in the Yellow Pages and get the highest quotes possible for written proof that the wall will cost $10,000. After obtaining quotes from the "neutral third party," you and the other side settle on an $8,000 discount on the home and the deal goes through. You get the wall fireproofed for $5,000 and profit $3,000 from the transaction.

Countermove: To break a deadlock with a neutral third party, bring in a third party that benefits you, not them. In the example of above, you brought in a high-priced contractor to get a big discount. The seller could have brought in a low priced contractor to benefit their argument. In court cases, both sides bring in "neutral" witnesses that will benefit their argument and their argument only. When negotiating to break a deadlock, bring in third parties that will further your cause.

Law #6: Create Dual Personalities for Contrast

Practical Gambit—Good Cop–Bad Cop

"You can't go to a negotiating table pointing a gun,
but you've got to keep it over your shoulder."

—JOE SLOVO

Without contrast there is no context. Ice cold water is only cold when contrasted with a glass of room temperature drinking water. Room temperature drinking water is cold relative to scalding hot boiling water. We need contrast to understand the value of things around us.

"There's no road map on how to raise a family:
it's always an enormous negotiation."

— MERYL STREEP

Through darkness we learn to see the light. Many children grow up with two parents, a mother and a father, and while one parent will play "nice," the other parent will play "disciplinarian." Often the mother will be the nice parent, and the father will give the children discipline. From the perspective of the children, there is a nice parent, one to confide in, one to find comfort, one to share their secrets with. The other parent can be seen as disciplinarian and can lay down the law when mother cannot. There are two roles to play, and this technique is called "Good cop–bad cop."

Practical Gambit—Good Cop–Bad Cop

"Negotiation is not a policy. It's a technique. It's something you use when it's to your advantage, and something that you don't use when it's not to your advantage."

—JOHN BOLTON

In Hollywood movies, we have become accustomed to "good cop–bad cop" during interrogation scenes. The bad cop will yell at his prisoner, call him scum, take away his comforts like cigarettes or coffee, and stare him down in a clear power play. Finally the bad cop will leave the room, unable to break his prisoner and the good cop will walk in. The good cop wants to "level" with his prisoner and understands his situation. He offers the prisoner a donut, a cup of coffee, and a cigarette. He'll even take off his tie, roll up his sleeves, and lean back to listen to what the prisoner has to say. The good cop is the prisoner's friend and on his side. If the prisoner will confide in the good cop, the bad cop won't come back again. But if the prisoner fails to confess his crimes to the good cop, they will send the bad cop back in for contrast. In reality, the good cop and bad cop are on the same team. They have the same motivation, agree on the same points, and are really the same person in a negotiation. A good cop and a bad cop are a team, and they operate as one and win together. Of course, being human, we feel an affinity towards the good cop and distaste towards the bad cop. With dual personalities, the contrast is what gives this strategy power. There is a place, an outlet, for the negotiators to be nice and to be human with one another. There is also an outlet for harshness, meanness, cruelty, and somewhat evil behavior through the bad cop. It may appear like the good cop and bad cop are not working together sometimes, but make no mistake, the good cop and bad cop are on the same side and typically are rehearsed in their positions and objectives.

Move: When negotiating with two people or a committee, one player on their side will act nicely and the other will act mean. In reality, they are both on the same side. Use this to your advantage to provide an outlet and positioning to make the upside of your offer even sweeter and the downside of your offer more nasty.

Example: Years ago when coaching a real estate student on buying homes at a discount I had a student who had just tied up a property under contract for purchase. The after-repair value of this home was $189,900 and he had a contract to purchase the home for $85,000. The sellers of the home were emotional—they must have inherited their wealth—and wanted to sell the home to open up their dream business—a bakery. Jason, my student, had negotiated a very low but fair price for the home of $85,000 with the knowledge that he was going to paint it, add some carpeting (likely less than $15,000 of renovations), and would make a stellar gross profit of $89,000. Jason wanted to show me the deal, so as his coach I went to see the house. Before we entered the house, I told him that I was going to be the bad cop, his renovation partner, and I was going to absolutely hate the house and hate the foundation. I told Jason we were going to ask for a concession before leaving and we would see how low we could get the price to go. After meeting the sellers at the home—they were very nice people—Jason walked the home and was very pleasant to the sellers. He had built a lot of rapport and comfort with them. I, on the other hand, found faults with the roof, and the foundation which looked somewhat questionable. After making a fuss about the roof and the foundation, I announced that the floor was sloping and Jason was paying "far too much" for this house. I announced that I hated the deal and told them I was going to wait in the car. Many minutes passed while I waited in the car. Finally, Jason walked out of the front door of the house and joined me in the car. "How much of a discount did you get?" I asked.

He replied "An additional $22,000 off of the purchase price! I'm now buying the house for $63,000!"

I couldn't believe that the sellers had given him such a steep concession! I was expecting an extra $2,000 or $5,000 off of the already low but fair price. Good cop–bad cop had worked its magic, and the fear of losing the deal by my bad-cop criticism had brought the sellers right down to their bottom line—fast!

Countermove: If you find the other side playing good cop–bad cop with you, call them out and say: "C'mon guys, you aren't gonna do that good cop–bad cop thing, are you?" Often identifying the tactic is enough to defuse it.

Countermove #2: Go over the good cop and bad cop's heads to their higher authority. If dealing with a realtor, call his broker. If dealing with appliance sales people, call the district manager. That will put a stop to good cop–bad cop immediately.

Countermove #3: Turn them both into bad cops by saying "Anything you say to me, I'm going to assume the other guy agrees!" Identify that you know they are working together and the game is over.

Law 7: Nothing Easy Is Good And Nothing Good Is Easy— Play Hard To Get

Practical Gambit—Never Take The First Offer

"I think each negotiation should be based on what's the best decision—taking everything into account, not taking one thing into account."

—Tony La Russa

As human beings we always want what we can't have. We have a deep-seated belief that valuable things are hard to get or rare. Diamonds are worth more than coal because they are supposedly more rare. Both are rocks, both are made of carbon, but diamonds are purposely kept in low supply by the international diamond brokers to increase their value. The same is true for fine art. Fine art is artificially manipulated with supply and demand to increase the value. Years ago I was an up-and-coming artist, and I consulted with a fine art dealer on how I could make a career. His reply was, "If you want to make it in the art world, you will have to purposely limit your supply of art or you will hurt your career." Real estate is no different. A single-family home on a nice street is a limited edition dwelling because of the limited-edition nature of the land that the building sits on, whereas a condo in the same area is worth less because you do not receive the limited-edition land underneath the condo unit. Limited edition drives up the value of an item. In many ways we believe that nothing easy is good, and nothing good is easy; we want value to be hard to get and hard to obtain, so to increase the value of your offer and value of your position, you must make your offer hard to get.

Move: Always reject the first offer to avoid buyer's remorse. People typically think that they could have done better when negotiating. Although studies show that no matter how good or how bad someone performs in a negotiation, they always think that they did their best. When an offer is easily accepted without any resistance, buyer's remorse will rear its ugly head: "I could have done better" will be ringing through their ears, and they may break the deal, walk away, or ask for another concession. To avoid this, make the other side feel like you are losing a little and that they have won—even if you are inclined to accept their first offer.

Example: You are selling a house for an asking price of $110,000. The other side offers you $100,000 for the property. You will accept $100,000 because you will walk away with a nice profit from a clean and quick sale. However, you counter at $105,000 to create resistance and an aura of value. You will slowly give away the $5,000 in concessions and will settle on $100,000 or even $101,000 or $102,000, and in the end you will comment on how good of a negotiator they are and that they "drive a hard bargain." The other side will feel elated that they received such a discount and you walk away with more than you bargained for. Had you accepted the quick $100,000, you may have spooked the other side, and they may have thought that the deal was too easy. People typically have intuition as to when they can ask for concessions or not; people who give concessions too freely and too quickly are perceived as weak. Do not be weak.

Countermove: As a general rule in negotiating, always challenge their position, their offers, and their counter offers for validity. When negotiating, challenge every price and every term to find resistance and sticking points. You can challenge on price, delivery, deposit, make, model, color, close date, terms and conditions, promises, extras, after-market add-ons, paint colors, and so on. In general, the more items you challenge, the more power you will have in the negotiation. You will also gain a sense of what is real and what is not real.

Law 8: Be Like Them—We Like People Who Are Like Us

Practical Gambit—Always Agree
"Feel, Felt, Found"

"Human beings are born solitary, but everywhere they are in chains—daisy chains—of interactivity. Social actions are makeshift forms, often courageous, sometimes ridiculous, always strange. And in a way, every social action is a negotiation, a compromise between 'his,' 'her' or 'their' wish and yours."

—ANDY WARHOL

"You really want to know how to stay alive? Get people to like you!"

—HAYMITCH, *THE HUNGER GAMES*

In a cocktail party with a large number of guests, there is an unwritten law that likes will attract likes. If you leave the people long enough, they will form into groups, and the groups will have certain commonalities. The businessmen will form a group, the stay-at-home moms will form a group, the engineers will form a group, the teenagers will form a group, and so on. This phenomenon is based on the fact that as humans, we like people who are like us. If you are going to meet, negotiate, and sell to a group of people, the easiest way to lower resistance to your ideas is to be like them!

Practical Gambit—Always Agree "Feel, Felt, Found"

"During a negotiation, it would be wise not to take anything personally. If you leave personalities out of it, you will be able to see opportunities more objectively."

—BRIAN KOSLOW

Move: In every negotiation there is some point of resistance, and where there is resistance, there is a competitive spirit. Perhaps you will disagree on price, perhaps you will disagree on delivery or deposits or some other mundane detail. What remains a powerful move in any negotiation is to always agree to defuse their competitive spirit! One technique to create commonality and agreement between two disagreeing parties is called the "feel, felt, found" method.

Example: The seller of a property wants $100,000 for his property and you can only pay $90,000 based on its current condition. You might say: "I understand how you *feel*, $100,000 is a nice number … I have *felt* in the past that I have wanted more for my properties too, but I found that the first offer I get is usually my best offer." Presenting your position from a feel, felt, found perspective makes it easier for the other side to agree because #1) you are agreeable in your disagreement, and #2) You are positioning your option as a story, which disarms the thinking brain.

Countermove: Should you find someone using "feel, felt, found" on you, simply agree with them and then challenge their position for validity. Understand that they are telling you a story and it may not have any validity at all. Alternatively, find a trade that would work for both sides.

Law #9: Humans Seek To Take Advantage Of Other Humans But Want To Avoid Being Taken Advantage Of

Practical Gambit—Dumb Is Smart and Smart Is Dumb

"What is negotiation but the accumulation of small lies leading to advantage?"

—FELIX DENNIS

Your ego is a bomb that must be diffused if you want to win when negotiating. There are four types of people: those who want to be liked, those who want to be comfortable, those who want to be right, and those who want to win. When negotiating, you must focus on winning, which means you will have to give up the need to be liked, the need to be comfortable, and the need to be right. In the end, it's okay to be wrong and still win. Too many negotiators fail in business and in life because they focus on being right and sacrifice the ability to win just to satisfy their own egos. To diffuse your ego and to keep your eyes on the prize, never forget when negotiating that smart is dumb and dumb is smart! Do not be alarmed by the idea of looking dumb; as the old saying goes, you will catch more flies with honey than with vinegar.

You typically are in a better position to conceal your intelligence, your information, and your position for as long as possible and perhaps never reveal it at all. To conceal your position and your intelligence is real power and power that can be used to gain an advantage later. Appearing to be dumb is infinitely more powerful when negotiating because in human nature, humans seek to take advantage of other humans but do not wish to be taken advantage of. Think about that for a moment. Human beings will endlessly take advantage of you if you let them. This is why we have consumer protection and laws to protect the weak and the stupid. In fact in the twenty-first century, it is usually better to appear to be dumb than to be smart. The next time you are in a drug store and need to find cough syrup, rather than reading the signs and trying to be smart, go to the front counter, tell the clerk you can't read, and that you need them to find cough syrup for you. In the modern world, we can no longer attack our fellow man on the grounds of being stupid, illiterate, slow, or dumb; instead, the clerk will have to respectfully walk you over to the cough syrup and will have to read the label for you.

When you appear to be dumber than you are, the ego of the other side may start to flex its muscles in front of you. People will carelessly reveal things to you that they should not have revealed because you appear to be too simple for them. You can also get away with repeating yourself, repeating your position, and strategically forgetting facts if you appear to be a little dumber than you are.

You may not be completely sold on appearing dumb in a negotiation, but let me offer you the opposite strategy. Imagine you walk into a negotiation as a know-it-all, or trying to appear smart, or having a PhD in the subject you are about to negotiate over. More often than not, the resentment and resistance of appearing more powerful than the other side will create obstacles that you never needed to overcome in the first place. Stay humble, stay dumb, conceal your position, and watch the other side give themselves away.

Move: People will make careless mistakes against opponents that they think to be less intelligent than them. Appear to be dumber and weaker than you are. Conceal your true power. Bill Bartmann, an American billionaire who shared a spot on the top entrepreneurs of all time with the likes of Henry Ford used to say "I can't read and have a poor memory." In fact, Bill Bartmann was a lawyer and CEO of a multi-billion dollar company, but by appearing to be dumb, he won over the hearts and minds of many people who found him to be approachable and an every day man.

Example: One of the most disarming phrases you can use in any negotiation is: "I'm new to this." By pleading ignorance and by offering your position of naïveté, you can get away with asking "stupid questions" that other people would normally gloss over, and you have the freedom to slow down the negotiation if you need to. Also, when you are *always* new to negotiating, it's an endless subject. As Ray Kroc, the founder of McDonalds, used to say, "It's good to be green; it means you are still growing."

Countermove: If you catch someone playing dumb, call them out on it. "You are smarter than that." "You know better!" Catch their ego and don't allow them to play dumb with you. Build up their ego to great heights and let them topple on their own weight.

Law #10: Why Buy the Cow if You Are Getting the Milk for Free?

Practical Gambit—Diminished Value of Services

"I'd like to add that negotiating is not something to be avoided or feared—it's an everyday part of life."

— LEIGH STEINBERG

There used to be an old wives' saying that made a case for saving sex until marriage. "Why buy the cow if you are getting the milk for free?" In the last century, it was common practice to remain a virgin until one married. The idea behind this was to consummate a marriage with sex for the first time was to bring love, sex, romance, and marriage together and pair bond two partners to each other. Since the sexual experience would be the only sexual experience both husband and wife experienced, it would be special and exclusive, and the odds of the marriage working out would be much higher. A saying that was said to young girls to discourage premarital sex was "why buy the cow if you are giving the milk away for free." When negotiating you must avoid giving the milk away for free because just like it is much harder to get married after having sex, it is also harder to collect on services that are already rendered.

Move: Services diminish in value rapidly after they are rendered. For example, every real estate salesperson has experienced their client asking for a discount on the realtor commission after the sales person has sold their home at a great price. People always think "the realtor didn't work very hard to sell my home, he spent five minutes with me and now I'm going to pay him 5 percent of my home?! I want a discount." In reality, the realtor may have performed a great service, diligently advertised the property, and put in much effort, energy, time, and money behind the scenes. But now that the pain of selling the home is gone, the client may try to betray his realtor. Such is the story of the scorpion and the frog in Aesop's fables: There once was a scorpion who wanted to cross a river, but he could not swim. The scorpion saw a frog by the river bank and called out to him "O Frog, I wish to cross the river, but I cannot swim. Can I climb on your back and you can ferry me across the water?" The frog replied, "Oh no! You are a scorpion, and if I let you onto my back, you will sting me and I will drown. I cannot take you across the water on my back!"

To which the scorpion replied, "No frog, I promise, I give you my word, I will not sting you, and we will both make it across the water safely."

At this, the frog believed the words of the scorpion and allowed the poisonous creature to climb onto his back. When the frog finally swam to the middle of the river with the scorpion on his back, he suddenly felt a sharp sting in his spine and poison rushed through his veins numbing his body into a slow paralysis. "Oh why, oh why did you sting me scorpion? I am becoming paralyzed with your poison, and now we both shall drown!" As the frog slowly sank into the water and the scorpion sank with him, the scorpion replied, "Because it is in my nature."

The scorpion and the frog is a dark story about human nature and also about services rendered. Whenever you are performing a service for someone else, especially an intangible service, negotiate payment up front and collect up front if possible. If you give a favor, collect up front if possible. People quickly forget the value of services that have happened in the past and quickly devalue them. To maintain full value, negotiate and collect up front.

To illustrate the intangible nature of services further, there once was a man who owned a printing press who was the publisher of a newspaper.

This printing press was enormous and took up an entire building in size. One day the printing press became, unaligned and the machine failed to work. The owner of the machine called a man who specialized in fixing machines just like his. After a few minutes of walking around the broken machine and surveying the damage, the repairman said "I can fix your machine, but it will cost you $10,000." To which the machine owner replied "$10,000 to have my machine fixed? I will gladly pay it, I am losing money by the minute every second that this machine is broken!"

"Okay" replied the repair man, "I will fix your machine for $10,000 right now" With saying this, he pulled a hammer out of his pocket and whacked the machine in just the right place. Almost by magic, the machine worked perfectly again and was printing newspapers as good as if it were brand new. The repairman started to write up the invoice for $10,000 and the machine owner, stunned said "I can't pay you $10,000 for one whack of a hammer! That is far too much money!" The machine owner then got a bright idea to attempt to pay less to the machine repair man. He said "Mr. Repairman, please write up your invoice with a detailed line by line breakdown of what the $10,000 is for" The machine owner thought he could get a discount if the repairman would break down his invoice to show where the $10,000 was being spent.

"No problem," replied the repairman as he proceeded to write up the invoice that read: Hammer whack $1.00 , knowing where to whack the hammer $9,999.00. After seeing this, the machine owner paid the repairman in full.

Example: A Realtor sells a house for 5 percent commission, and then the homeowner tries to cut the realtor's commission from 5 percent down to 3 percent after the realtor has done the hard work of selling the home. The home owner will say "Mr. Realtor, you are making too much money; it was too easy for you. I don't want to pay you your full value." Any intangible service must be protected with a written agreement up front and payment up front if possible; otherwise, services will diminish in value the longer they go unpaid.

Countermove: Negotiate your fees and services up front or receive concessions and trades up front. Do not let time pass between your value rendered and client payment.

Law #11: Fear of Loss Is Greater Than the Promise of Gain

Practical Gambit—Walk-Away Power

"The way to love anything is to realize that it might be lost."

—G. K. Chesterton

"Anything not saved will be lost"

—Nintendo

Human beings are generally motivated by two things: pleasure and pain. We either want to move towards pleasure or move further away from pain. Likewise, just like pleasure and pain, we are also motivated by the opportunity to gain by taking a chance or the fear of loss. As a species, we generally survive by conserving energy and avoiding loss. It is human nature to conserve energy, effort, time, and money and save our resources for when our survival is on the line. In the days of cave men, we would lie around in caves, conserving energy in case a lion, tiger, or bear would attack us, and then with our stored energy we would run away. When it comes to negotiating or trading, fear of loss is always more powerful than the promise of gain. If you can understand how to motivate others by scarcity and potential of loss rather than promising gain, you will almost always gain the upper hand in a negotiation. Most people are functioning below a self-actualized level and operate from a place of fear and scarcity. To communicate in terms of scarcity will stimulate the lower parts of the human brain, the reptile and mammalian parts, and will drive decision making. Fear of loss always outweighs the promise of gain, especially when you communicate directly to the reptilian brain.

Scarcity and fear of loss is so powerful that it can be completely paralyzing, even when we are surrounded by abundance. There once was a little old lady who wanted to cross the ocean in a cruise ship. She saved up all of her money and bought herself some cheap Wonder Bread and little cans of tuna to sustain her on her voyage. She was able to save up enough money to barely afford the cheapest ticket on the cruise and because she hardly had any money left over, she kept her cans of tuna fish and loaves of Wonder Bread close to her and rationed her food as she crossed the ocean. She stayed in her cabin for the entire voyage and began to fear that her rations would run out. If she ran out of tuna fish and Wonder Bread, she would starve and might not survive the voyage! Finally the cruise ship crossed the ocean, and she opened the door to her cabin and right outside her quarters was the biggest, most luxurious buffet known to man. This buffet was abundantly stocked with cheese plates, fruit plates, vegetable platters, roast meats, sweet breads, chocolate fountains, and absolutely any food that the heart would desire. As she marveled at the abundance of food that had been outside her cabin door all along, the buffet manager looked over at her and said, "This buffet was included with your ticket madam; help yourself!"

Why didn't the little old lady bother to open the door to her cabin and take a look outside? In this story, there is unlimited abundance available to us, but our scarcity mindsets limit our thinking to believe that we are operating with finite resources. In truth, everything you need or want in life is owned or controlled by someone else, and the world truly is abundant, if you can look past your fear of loss and scarcity mentality.

When negotiating only 2.5 percent of the population consists of self-actualized individuals who are self-aware to understand what they need and want. The other 97.5 percent are not self-actualized and will be motivated by scarcity and fear of loss versus the promise of gain. Appeal to this common human fear when negotiating, and you will have the advantage more often than not.

Practical Gambit—Walk-Away Power

"I hope everybody will go back to the negotiating table. I've always said this is the only way forward."

—MOHAMED ELBARADEI

Move: There is always pressure in any negotiation. One side has pressure to buy; the other side has pressure to sell, and both sides can use scarcity to their advantage. Scarcity in the modern world is mostly artifically created or perceived rather than real. We have so much abundance in the marketplace now with access to a global market via the internet, there is a glut of opportunity. Nonetheless, fear of loss is always more powerful than the promise of gain, so exploit this human fear to gain advantage. Always be prepared to walk away from the bargaining table to create scarcity. Just as in love, the one who cares less has all the power. By being able to walk away and make your offer scarce, there is much more leverage in having an indifferent attitude over being needy. Need and power are inverse—the more you need something, the less power you have. There is no such thing as a must-have investment, must-have house, or must-have relationship.

Example: Nothing is more powerful than walking away from a deal in deadlock where both sides cannot agree on a price. If you are deadlocked on price or any other item or term, start to walk away very slowly and start the car. Sit in the car for a few minutes before driving away, and very often the fear of loss will make the other party chase you. This is no different than a cat and mouse or a fisherman and a fish. Negotiation is push and pull, give and take. Most negotiations or sales come down to a yes or no decision at the end "to be or not to be." If they will not give you a yes, force a no and begin to walk away. If your offer has enough value, they will come back to you because fear of loss is greater than the opportunity for gain. As the old adage says, "A bird in the hand is better than two in the bush."

Countermove: The most powerful counter to -way power is to open multiple negotiations simaltaneously. In the words of Grant Cardone, have ten deals going for every one that you need to close. Have multiple deals, multiple options open at all times, and very rarely offer exclusivity unless you have massive upside. If you have ten deals under negotiation for every one that you need, you will not succumb to the fear of loss when the other side tries to use walk-away power on you. In negotiating, sales, and business, the one with the greater numbers usually wins. When it comes to numbers, think of the male and female reproductive strategies and consider your position. A man produces 72,000,000 sperm a day to reproduce and a woman produces one egg a month. In a tribal society, groups of 150 or less humans, the king has access to over 50 percent of the women; he is not reliant on any one relationship for reproductive success. On the other hand, the women in the tribe produce one egg a month and should they become fertilized by one man, they are somewhat dependent for at least nine months while pregnant and for some number of years while the baby is young. Women need exclusivity when it comes to reproduction, but men do not. When it comes to negotiating and deals, make sure you have more options and more deals. Do not get stuck in exclusivity unless the deal is too good to pass up.

Law #12: The Law of Reciprocity

Practical Gambit—Trade-Off Principle and Unfair Trading

Pay every debt, as if God wrote the bill.

—Ralph Waldo Emerson

I n kindergarten we learn the golden rule: Do unto others as you would have them do unto you. In plain English, treat other people the way you want to be treated. As human beings, we have an unwritten law of reciprocity and some sort of belief in karma: what goes around comes around. To illustrate this, we have the law of reciprocity. We have a general common belief that we should reciprocate when others give to us. If we receive a gift, we feel obligated to give a gift. When someone pays it forward to us, we want to it forward to the next person. Reciprocity, give and take, is one of the human fundamentals of trade, and we somewhat assume that trading and reciprocity should be fair.

Four Levels of Exchange

With reciprocity, there are four levels of human exchange, and to become a better negotiator, you must understand the four levels of exchange to maximize your effectiveness.

Abundant exchange: You put in $1 and get $5 of value. This is the relationship that everyone dreams of. Both sides are giving, and every time a gift is given, you receive in a bigger and bigger way. Very few relationships are abundant in this nature.

Fair exchange: You put in $1 and receive $1 back. Most businesses and people operate with fair exchange. You receive what you expect, no more no less.

Partial exchange: You put in $1 and receive $0.50 back. You may feel cheated, you may complain, you may never use that business or service ever again, but it's not the worst-case scenario.

Criminal exchange: You put in $1 and receive $0.00 back in return. These people and businesses that take freely and give nothing must be avoided at all costs, and should you encounter a criminal exchange person or business, turn and run the other way. These people will steal life, and the more you give to them, the more they will take from you.

With reciprocity, most people expect a fair exchange, a fair trade. Tit for tat. "You do this for me, I'll do this for you." "You scratch my back, I'll scratch yours." Often when bargaining or negotiating, people expect fair trades, and if you give, you will typically receive.

To get more, you must give more, and that is where abundant exchange exists. You may give abundantly to the marketplace through free content, free education, free gifts, beautiful presentation, samples and so on, and typically those who give the greatest also receive the greatest. Such is the law of reciprocity. I used to work for the fortieth fastest-growing company in Canada, and the marketing plan was simple: Give more free education to the market than anyone else. We gave more and received more in return. The company did millions of dollars of sales overnight.

When negotiating you may want to use all four levels of exchange: abundant, fair, partial, and criminal to your advantage. There are different times for different types of reciprocity and exchange just like there are different sauces and spices for food. As a negotiator, you need to know when to use each type of exchange and what will bring you the greatest effectiveness in the field.

Practical Gambit—Trade-Off Principle and Unfair Trading

"Of course as a small country you're not necessarily in the strongest negotiating position unless you're negotiating with other small countries."

—HELEN CLARK

Move: Very simply, most people understand the concept of trading. When they ask for something, you ask for something in return. This type of trading is "tit for tat" and may be equal or unequal.

Example: When I flip and sell my residential homes to the public, if the buyers want a cheaper price, I will simply take the appliances out of the deal and offer a token concession. In actuality, I am not offering any discount, just shuffling numbers around to make the other side feel like they are trading for real value. When trading you will see the greatest gains when you trade unequally in your favor.

Countermove: Make a fuss about the trades that they ask for and when you trade, trade in unequal value. When they ask for one thing, ask for three or four things in return. Most people are unfocused on the small points and will only be focused on three or four major points in any given negotiation. You can capture a lot of bonus items by simply asking for more concessions on every unfair trade. Give them things that are at no cost for you, but high in perceived value. For example, a home seller may value a bigger deposit to show a stronger buying intention. As a buyer, the deposit size truly doesn't matter, so you can offer a larger deposit and demand a lower price and other concessions in return.

Law #13: Exploit Prizes and the Competitive Nature of Humanity

Practical Gambit—The Crunch—You'll Have to Do Better Than That!

Inside of every human being is a competitive spirit and the desire to win. Everyone loves to win, everyone loves to win a prize, and the harder it is to win, the more highly we value the prize. When negotiating, our egos and competitive nature can overtake us in the moment and at times, the desire to win, compete, or have our way will overcome all other emotions and logic.

During the Dutch golden age, there was such a demand for tulip bulbs that the price to possess one tulip bulb shot up exponentially overnight. People had such a desire to compete and to win a tulip bulb that in some cases, people were trading their homes just to possess one tulip bulb. Of course, the market eventually became flooded, and tulips became common, and the prize was gone. But in the moment, there was an emotional frenzy to win the prize of the day—the tulip bulb.

As a negotiator you want to exploit the feeling of prizes and competitive nature of humanity to make your offer look much more appealing. Can you make your offer hard to get? Can you make your offer more exclusive? Are there requirements to be chosen for such an offer? Do you need to apply to get in? Ivy League schools like Harvard are not better schools based on curriculum or merit. They are simply better schools because they only accept the best students, and naturally a high concentration of the best students will create a top-notch school. In reality, those students—the prize—could move to any school, and the school would become great. They don't have to be at Harvard to be great. But the reality is, the competitive nature, the high requirements to get into Harvard, and the high cost creates a demand and a prize that millions of competitive students aspire to possess.

When negotiating exploit the human need to win the prize and make the other side feel selected or chosen to make your offer special.

Practical Gambit—The Crunch—You'll Have to Do Better Than That!

Move: Much as a cat with a ball of yarn, the cat will chase the ball of yarn, and if you yank the ball further, the cat will leap further. When the other side makes a proposal you can simply reply, "You'll have to do better than that!" This will incite the other side to chase the prize and potentially negotiate against themselves. Another powerful phrase to bring out the competitive spirit is, "You're close, but I know you can do better." Everyone wants to win, and being close is not enough!

Example: Often a skilled realtor will receive a verbal offer for less than full asking price. A skilled realtor will often say immediately to the verbal offer, "You will have to do better before I will even present that to my client." Setting the expectation up front for a "better offer" will usually strip most unsophisticated negotiators of their position, and many buyers will end up paying close to full price.

Countermove: A common countermove to the other side telling you that you will have to do better is to nail down exactly, "How much better?" When they are vague, you need to quantify. When they want you to quantify, be vague. Hold this double standard for great success.

Law #14: Humans Assume That Everything Written Down Is True
Practical Gambit: Power of the Written Word

The Bible is often called "the book." It is the #1 most influential book in America and in fact, Bible comes from the Greek word *biblio*, which means book. The Bible is considered to be literally true in many circles because "if it is written down in a book, it must be true." Such is the power of the written word that the most influential book in America happens to be called "the book" because it was in fact the only book accessible in Europe for nearly 2,000 years. Until the Renaissance in the 1600s there were no books available for the average person to read. Most information was kept on animal skins and parchment was very expensive to produce and reproduce. All text had to be reproduced by hand, which took years to produce by very skilled hands as most of the population was illiterate. When the Renaissance swept through Europe in the 1600s, a new invention was at the forefront of the "rebirth" of Europe—the printing press. Suddenly, the average man could actually read the only book that was being printed—the Bible, which was the ruling literature in Europe for nearly 2,000 years. For the first time, the average man could check and read the words printed inside of the Bible. Up to this point, the written word was kept hidden away from the public and was transmitted orally through cardinals and bishops who may have been illiterate themselves and would orally transmit the information in "the book," which they may or may not have had.

The written word has always been powerful to human beings, in fact so powerful that the written word can even be from God himself (capital G or not). When God gave Moses the Ten Commandments, he carved them into stone tablets. They say that words are more powerful than drugs because drugs will wear off after they pass through the blood stream, but words will stick with you for years. Tell a man he's a failure, and he may believe you for life and become a failure. Tell the same man he is a success and he may believe you and become a success. Such is the power of the spoken word and the written word.

When negotiating, the written word is always one of the most powerful tools that anyone can use for or against you. Any religion of the world whether it be Christianity, Judaism, Islam, or even new religions like Scientology have their roots in "a book" or series of books—written words to reinforce philosophies of life.

As humans we understand the value of a book and the written word, and we know that it takes immense resources and planning along with fact checking to get a book into print. There is a mystical power to the written word, and when we see it, we believe its validity almost instantaneously. The laws of the land are written, and so we believe them. If they are not written, they would be very difficult to enforce. For the palest ink is more powerful than the strongest memory.

Use the power of the written word to your advantage, just as the rulers of every great civilization of the past have. When a civilization goes through a regime change or revolution, they burn the books and edit the history of the past to suit the present and the future. Such is the power of the written word to control the past, present, and future.

Move: People have a need to feel that the written words that they see in front of them are true. When negotiating bring as much written literature to support your case as possible. Bring market statistics, brochures, books, published materials, and anything else that strengthens your case in writing. If it's written in a book, it must be true! Of course this may or may not be true, but it's always harder to challenge the written word and ink on a page.

Example: Home prices when advertised in the newspaper or on the Multiple Listing Service are often perceived as "facts." An advertised price of any item is not a fact but always an opinion. Until someone is prepared to pay the asking price, the asking price is not real until payment is collected. Asking prices are opinions and not facts.

Countermove: Challenge the written word for validity and ask for sources where the information is derived from. To completely counter the written word, bring your own written materials into the negotiation or manufacture your own written word in advance.

Law #15: Create Value Through Loss

Practical Gambit: The Withdrawn Offer

As human beings we often don't see value in things until we lose them. The things we have in our possession we often take for granted be it our health, the paycheck we get at our job every two weeks, our spouse, our children, or our country that we live in. Only when we lose something do we see value.

McDonald's is a world-famous restaurant that sells cheap fast and delicious food, namely cheeseburgers, hamburgers, fries, and shakes. The company is always innovating by introducing new foods to the menu with limited time offerings. The beauty of a limited time offering is that the crocodile brain is programmed to look for and see new things. The word new is an ever-powerful word in marketing, because our brains are hardwired to look for things that are new in our environment. The McRib is a sandwich made of spinal cords and other pork entrails that are ground up into a rib-like patty, covered in barbeque sauce and served on a McDonald's bun. The McRib is not a popular enough sandwich to be on the menu every day at McDonald's; not enough people want the sandwich to sustain long-term sales. However, the McRib is sold once a year on a limited-time sale and because it is a limited-time offer that will disappear soon, the McRib has strong enough sales to warrant a once-a-year offering. Make no mistake, the McRib is not a great sandwich like the Big Mac—it can't stay on the menu forever—but because of the artificially limited nature of the offering, there is value to the customer.

In real estate it is customary for buyers to put an expiration date and time on their offers when purchasing a property. This offer shall be valid until such day and such time, after which it is no longer valid. Companies also put time limits on direct mail offerings and coupons in the mail: "Must be used by a certain date or invalid." In reality, many businesses will honor a deal they made in the past if you ask the management, and the limited-time offer is just a ploy to get the consumer to take action, but it works because value is created through loss.

Practical Gambit: The Withdrawn Offer

Move: When negotiating you may reach a point where the other side is being difficult, but you know they want to do business with you. In that case you simply withdraw your offer and let them chase you.

Example: The other side is agreeing on all major points but asking for more concessions. They are pushing the envelope too far and you know they are committed to doing business. You take your offer off the table and let them chase you. This will eliminate much of the haggling for more concessions and will increase the value of your previous offer.

Countermove: When the otherside withdraws their offer on you either (1) Take the best offer or (2) walk away and call their bluff. Sometimes this can be a game of chicken, and egos can flare when both sides walk away. Typically in negotiating, ultimatums don't work due to their inflexibility, and if you are challenged on your ultimatum and lose, you typically lose all of your power. Always have a backup if you are going to walk away from a withdrawn offer.

Law #16: Make Them Feel Like They Won

Practical Gambit: Positioning For Easy Acceptance

"If you want deals, go to Wal-Mart!"

—TONY MARTONE, REALTOR, TO BUYERS WHO
ASK FOR A DISCOUNT ON HIS HOMES.

No matter how much you win in any negotiation, always make the other side feel like they won. Everyone wants to come out a winner, and studies have shown that no matter how good or bad someone performs in a negotiation, they always feel like they did their best. There is always an instinct to celebrate or brag when you get your key points in any negotiation, but hold the celebration until you are far away from the other party and they cannot see or hear you celebrating. No matter what, always make the other side feel like they drove a hard bargain and that they are winning a good deal by being great negotiatiors. This will limit buyer's remorse, cancellations, and people going back on previous deals trying to get more concessions. Reward the other side by saying, "You drive a hard bargain, but I'll accept your offer," "You are a great negotiator, and you got me on this one!," "I can't believe I'm giving you this deal but ..." and so on. The more they feel like they won, the more solid your final agreement will be.

Practical Gambit: Positioning For Easy Acceptance

Move: Save a small concession to satisfy the ego of the other side. Your offer may be fair and may satisfy the price and terms of the other side, but their ego may not be satisifed by making such an easy deal. Do not open with your best offer to give yourself some room for concessions and save a few small concessions for the very end to make them feel like they won.

Example: You and the other side have made an agreement on price and terms; however, there is still some final resistance because the ego of the other side doesn't feel like they made a good enough deal. Make them feel good about giving in to you. At the last minute, you save a very small concession that, should they take your offer right now, you will give them something extra to satisfy their ego and make it easy to say "yes" to your offer. Disarm their ego and make it easy for them to say yes.

Countermove: When the other side is positioning you for easy acceptance by giving you last-minute concessions to pressure you into a deal, ignore the easy concessions and focus on the main issues. The small concessions are often immaterial and a decoy to distract you from the more important issues.

Law #17: He Who Writes The Rules Wins The Game

Practical Gambit: Always Be The One To Write The Contract

The golden rule: He who has the gold makes the rules

The golden rule: He who writes the rules, gets the gold

—Robert Kiyosaki

In the game of Monopoly, players start out with a handful of money and move around the board game buying up properties, green houses, and red hotels. The players are playing the game, and when a player runs out of money, he is out of the game. One player is the bank, and the bank writes the rules of the game. The bank cannot run out of money and in the written rules of the game:

> *The Bank never "goes broke." If the Bank runs out of money, it may issue as much more as may be needed by merely writing on any ordinary piece of paper.—Rule from the game of Monopoly*

The bank writes the rules of the game and because the rules are written by the bank, the bank cannot lose!

The same principles apply to human nature and deal making in general. The person who makes the rules always has an advantage, and the person who controls the written contracts and literature always has an advantage over those who do not. The most powerful institutions in our modern society, religion, government, the courts, and the banks all create written rules for other people that are made by them to control you. If you write the rules, you win the game.

Practical Gambit: Always Be The One To Write The Contract

Move: Always be the one who controls the contracts and the written documents in a negotiation. If you control the documents, you also control the small details that may be overlooked. If you control the contracts you can slant the deal in your favor through minor details that add up to a major advantage.

"What the big print giveth, the small print taketh away."
—GEORGE ROSS

Example: Get control of the written contracts in the negotiation by suggesting: "I'll have my lawyer do the paperwork to save us both some money."

Countermove: The pen is mightier than the sword. Should the other side try to control the negotiation with their own written contracts and fine print, simply sit down with a pen and cross out and initial the small details you do not agree with. This positions you to take control of the written word and brings the power back into your hands.

Law 18: The Caveman Principle—Humans Are Inherently Lazy

Practical Gambit: The Done-for-You Technique

O ne of the fundamentals of human nature is that humans are inherently lazy. Most people are essentially cave men who want to lie around in their caves all day conserving energy just in case they may need their energy for survival later. Modern man does not live in caves anymore, but he will sit in the darkness of his apartment watching TV and eating pizza until he runs out of money and has to go back to work, much like the cave man who will lie around in his cave by the fire until he runs out of food and has to go hunting again. We can evolve, but human nature is still the same throughout the ages; we are lazy and won't spend time, money, effort, or energy unless we have to. It is because of this caveman nature and an unwillingness to spend our energy that leaves most of the American population fat, broke, and uneducated. To be fit, wealthy, and educated all require an expenditure of energy and an investment that most people do not want to make. If you understand the lazy nature of people, you can exploit this need to conserve energy to your advantage.

Practical Gambit: The Done-for-You Technique

Move: Exploit the need to be lazy by doing all of the work in advance. When you make your offer, have everything "done for you"—send a fully finished contract, filled out, with a check attached and just needing their signature. The easier you can make it for the caveman on the other side of the table, the less resistance you will have in getting to yes.

Example: Some of the strongest offers you can make are where you can skip the verbal haggling and open up with a pre-filled out offer, check attached, and just requiring a single signature to make the deal official. Skipping the verbal offer and going straight to the written can be a very powerful starting point, and can give you massive starting leverage in any deal.

Countermove: If someone approaches you with a done-for-you offer, either have your team redo the offer in your favor (an expenditure of time and money) or read it carefully and cross out and initial small points you don't like before accepting. A done-for-you offer is typically not in your favor, and you will always pay a premium for being lazy.

Law 19: Humans Turn Nonsense into Meaning and Meaning into Nonsense

Practical Gambit: Funny Money

O ne of the most amazing talents of the human race is our ability to add meaning to things that seemingly have no meaning at all. Consider fine art—paint on a canvas: because of the rarity or artists name or supply and demand, paint on canvases can trade for thousands, millions, or even hundreds of millions of dollars. We have projected meaning onto a meaningless canvass and in return created value. The same mechanism of the brain that can add meaning to meaningless things can also take meaningful things and degrade them into nonsense.

It has been documented in history that the American Indians "sold" the island of Manhattan in New York for $24 worth of glass beads and bobbles. The island of Manhattan in 1996 Manhattan Island's estimated worth was $34,000,000,000. The land was the American Indians' way of life and ultimately meaningful: they hunted, fished, and lived on that island. Instead they traded a very important vital piece of land and a way of life for $24 of nonsense.

The mechanism in the brain that allows us to place meaning on things is extremely powerful and ultimately a double-edged sword. Understand that meaning can be added to items of little value like trinkets and glass beads and meaning can also be stripped away from items of true value like land, gold, or time.

If you can manipulate the meaning of items in a negotiation, you will ultimately come out on top.

Practical Gambit: Funny Money

Move: Casinos have understood for years that gamblers playing with meaningless chips will spend more than if they were playing the same games with meaningful cash. This is one way of creating "funny money" and stripping the meaning away from real value and creating nonsense in the process.

Car dealerships at the time of writing this book no longer post the actual price of a car for purchase and instead post the bi-weekly payment after financing. Instead of talking about real money or buying a car for $35,000, the dealership has trained its sales people to talk about $132 bi-weekly so it's much harder to negotiate the true price and cut through the nonsense of funny money. Real money is $35,000 for the car, cash today; funny money is $132 bi-weekly. When you are talking about funny money, or the $132 bi-weekly, you have no idea what the real price is or the terms of the loan. Most consumers will accept funny money when negotiating and won't pay attention to the real money at stake or the $35,000 sticker price.

Example: Realtors will use funny money when selling houses all the time. Instead of talking about a $115,000 house, the real estate salesperson will sell his clients on $499/month. Who cares if the client pays $115,000 or $100,000? "The difference in the monthly payment is only a few dollars." Many salespeople will sell using funny money instead of real money, especially when financing is available for houses, cars, appliances, and other major purchases.

Countermove: Do not accept funny money when buying or selling. Always bring the money back into REAL money terms; do not accept funny money unless it is to your advantage.

Law 20: Create Clutter and Let Them Sort It Out

Practical Gambit: The Decoy

Although the human mind is more powerful than any computer that man has ever been able to build, the human mind has many weaknesses when bargaining and negotiating with complex situations. One limitation of the thinking brain is that the neocortex, the mind's eye, can only focus on one thing at a time. There is no such thing as multi-tasking, which is multi-stupid and in reality, multi-tasking is just rapidly switching your focus from one item to another. When negotiating there is usually one major point such as price or perhaps a term that a buyer or seller truly wants and then there are likely three minor points that the buyer or seller truly wants. Everything else is immaterial. There is one major point and three minor points in almost every negotiation or situation. The human brain can't really grasp more than one major point and three minor points because the mind can only focus on one item at time.

One way to gain power in a negotiation is to raise issues and create items that may or may not be important, which is called clutter. When you can add extra clutter and raise extra issues in a negotiation, you become the one with more items to trade. Since every negotiation will boil down to trading at some point, you might as well be the person with more items to trade. Typically the person with more items to trade is usually the person who comes out on top.

If the average person is going to fixate on one major item and 3 minor items, make sure you raise 10 issues in your negotiation so that you can give many of your items away and still come out ahead.

Practical Gambit: The Decoy

Move: Take the other side's mind off the ball by adding clutter: nonsense decoy items to the negotiation.

Example: You may want a $20,000 discount off of the asking price when purchasing a house, but instead of simply asking for $20,000 less, you will ask for (1) a $20,000 discount, (2) a possession date six months in the future, (3) a fresh coat of paint on the interior of the house, (4) all junk removed from the garage, (5) A small deposit of $1,000 to secure the deal, and (6) all brand-new appliances delivered from the store of your choice. In reality you only want a $20,000 discount but you are asking for six items of clutter, and when looking at your offer, the other side will ultimately concede on some pieces of clutter but will give you other terms for free. When you ask for more than you need, you will always have more to give away when it comes to trading. Typically the side with more to trade is the side that wins in any negotiation.

Countermove: To eliminate clutter and find the one major point and three minor points, simply challenge every single demand for validity. When you challenge each item and counter on the small points, you will quickly find out which points are nonsense and which are real. The other side will give you resistance on the real issues and the nonsense items will fall away as if they never existed.

Law 21: Emotion Will Always Overpower Logic

Practical Gambit: Put Them in the Driver's Seat

In the human brain, there are three brains to bargain with. The neo-cortex, the thinking brain is ruled by the less evolved mammalian brain also known as the emotional brain. The emotional brain is ruled by the reptilian brain, which is connected to the limbic system and responsible for primitive functions such as breathing, eating, and staying alive. As the most evolved species on the planet Earth we seem to think sometimes that we are rational creatures and that we "think" about our decisions. Very often a salesperson looking to make a sale will hear his prospect say, "Let me think about it," when in reality, there is nothing to think about. What "let me think about it" means is that he does not have enough information to make a decision. In the end, human decisions are based on emotions and not logic. The primitive parts of the brain rule the thinking parts, and that is why smart people do dumb things. As one of my mentors used to say, "When emotions go up, thinking goes down."

If you understand that decision making is made almost exclusively with emotion and how we "feel" about a certain situation, you will see value in the ability to communicate in such a way to control the feelings that other people have about your offer.

People make decisions based on emotion but justify with logic. Learn to manipulate the emotions of the other side through questions, stories, and the ability to paint pictures in the other side's mind, and you will more often than not win what you want in business and in life.

Practical Gambit: Put Them in the Driver's Seat

Move: To create emotion and feelings in your negotiation ask questions to control the mind of your opponent. Get them emotionally involved in the decision and put them in the driver's seat. Ask: "Five years from now, looking back on this decision, how will it feel to have this solved today?" Or, "Had you made this decision ten years ago, how would your life be different today?" Both of those questions take the prospect and move him into a moment in time and put him in the driver's seat where he can feel what it would be like to have the right outcome.

Example: When selling homes, often the homes are staged with furniture, art, wine, candles, travel items, the new clean smell, and a fresh coat of paint. The home buyers fall in love with the lifestyle they feel when they walk into the home and ultimately get attached to the emotional feeling that the staging items bring. People don't buy houses; they buy lifestyle. In reality, after the couple moves into the new home, their furniture looks not nearly as good as the staging furniture, and the home will never look as good as when it was staged, but the fantasy and feeling of the perfect life and the perfect home is what creates a strong buying decision and a desire to pay full price for the feeling and the potential lifestyle. Many of the homes I have flipped in the past that have been beautifully staged often sell for record high prices when I sell them and years later sell for less because the resellers can't create the same feeling or lifestyle that they had when they purchased.

Countermove: Focus on the real issues; don't get emotionally wrapped up in the feelings. Have your desired outcome written down in advance and a list of things you will give and not give. Staying rational and writing down your major points will keep you from getting emotional. It may also help to bring an outside advisor who is not emotional about your decision to keep you from getting to emotional in a negotiation. Often someone with nothing to gain or lose is a great counterbalance to you should you become emotional when negotiating.

Law 22: Big Lies Are More Believable Than Small Lies

Practical Gambit: Open with an Extreme Position, Ask For The Moon

Where all think alike, no one thinks very much.

—WALTER LIIPPMANN

The term con man is an American term short for confidence trick or confidence scam. A con man will build up the confidence of his victim into buying into his scheme, and once he has the victim's money he disappears.

In 1925, Victor Lustig a con artist in Paris read an article in the newspaper about how the Eiffel tower was in disrepair and that even the paint was too expensive to maintain. The tower itself was intended to be moved somewhere else by 1909 but instead the Parisian government left the structure standing. Sensing opportunity, Lustig called himself the deputy director-general of the Ministry of Posts and Telegraphs and called six of the biggest scrap dealers in Paris to obtain bids to sell the tower for scrap. Due to public outcry, Lustig insisted that the business dealing be kept secret and that the scrap dealers must not mention the tower or the bidding to anyone else. He then had the six scrap dealers taken in a limousine to the Eiffel tower to walk the property and gauge which of his victims was most eager and vulnerable to his trick.

Lustig could sense which scrap dealer was going to be his bidder: Andre Poisson, who was insecure and wished to break into the Parisian business scene by dismantling the Eiffel tower. Although Poisson's wife was suspicious of the deal, the secrecy, and the speed, Lustig mentioned in secret to Poisson that he was not making the money he desired as a government official and that he wished he had a much better lifestyle. Poisson understood immediately that Lustig was a corrupt government official and that he was asking for a bribe. In addition to receiving a very large bribe to win the contract, Lustig also made off with a suitcase full of cash for selling the Eiffel tower for scrap. Poisson was so ashamed that he had been tricked that he did not complain to the police.

A month later, Lustig returned to Paris to run the scam again with six new scrap dealers. This time the police were alerted, but Lustig evaded arrest.

The human mind is more vulnerable to a big lie than a small lie. When something is extreme, very large, or very small, it can be so crazy that we have to believe it. Professional negotiators know that opening with a modest position or asking for modest concessions in a negotiation will yield few results in the long run. It is much better to open with an extreme position and ask for extreme concessions that, by a failure of logic, are more believable to the human mind.

Practical Gambit: Open with an Extreme Position, Ask For The Moon

Negotiators who open with extreme positions almost always outperform negotiators who open with modest positions. By sheer size of a demand, you have more room to concede your offer and more power by being bold. By being so bold and so confident, the other side, which is unable to differentiate between a real extreme demand and a made-up extreme demand, will have to spend energy and negotiate you out of your extreme position to a realistic one. You have an advantage with your extreme position in that you are asking for so much right away that it will take a lot of energy to bring you back into line.

Move: Ask for more than you know you will get. A student and friend of mine named Sean is a professional real estate investor who purchases distressed properties from distressed owners at an extreme discount. When negotiating with a distressed property owner, he will bring written evidence and comparable homes that have sold for "tear down" prices known as land value. Since Sean opens his negotiation at land value or below land value, he is able to purchase his homes at an extreme discount. He recently purchased a property for $24,000 that could immediately appraise at $100,000 by using this technique. Opening with extreme positions yields extreme results in your favor.

Example: Offer land value or a "tear down" price (land value minus demolition) for a distressed home that you are about to buy. Perhaps land value is $40,000 and market value is $100,000. There is nothing wrong with opening in an extremely low position or extremely high position and giving up ground to the other side. They will feel like they won something by bringing you from an extreme position to a more realistic spot. If you do not open with an extreme position, you will be leaving far too much money on the table and will never know where the bottom line really is. This technique is very important for nearly all types of negotiations. Caution: Be careful with this technique because opening in an extreme position may destroy your credibility in the process. If you are going to ask for something extreme, have the credibility to back up your offer with hard data or facts. Otherwise you will be viewed as a "tire kicker" and not a serious buyer or seller. For example, making an extremely low offer on a home at $60,000 when the asking price is $100,000 may be frowned upon when you give a deposit of $1000. But if you make the same offer of $60,000 with a deposit of $60,000 cash and a closing date twenty-four hours from now, the extreme position of a large deposit and quick close will have a much higher chance of success and will be so crazy that the buyer will believe your buying power over the $1000 deposit on the same offer. Many lawyers cannot even process a property purchase in twenty-four hours, and the other side will likely ask you to slow the deal down. Using an extreme position will catch the other side off balance and will keep the other side reactive to your proactive approach.

Countermove: When the other side opens with an extreme position, you may counter in an extreme position and challenge every single point of their offer. There is nothing wrong with meeting an extreme offer with an extreme counter offer to challenge the other side's credibility. The winner of the negotiation typically is the person who opens with an extreme offer followed by small concessions over time. Typically the person who gives the first big concession loses and professional negotiators know to monitor the "rate of concession," also known as the rate at which things are given away. A negotiator who begins to give fast and big concessions shows a sign of weakness by doing so, and professional negotiators will take advantage of such weakness.

Law 23: Need and Power Have an Inverse Relationship

Practical Gambit: The Apathetic Buyer

The opposite of power is need. The more needy you are, the less power you have. The less needy you are, the more power you have. Power is important in negotiating. In general, power is the ability to get things done. Someone with little power has a high degree of need, and someone with a high degree of power will have a low degree of need. Power and need are inverse in that the more you have of one, the less you have of the other. To be a powerful negotiator you must rely on as few people as possible and have as few needs as possible.

There are two types of items in negotiation—needs and wants. Typically a negotiator will have one need and three wants in any such negotiation. There may be price, terms, deposits, delivery terms, financing, speed of service, return policy, color, and options on the table for any given nego- tiation, and typically there is one major need on both sides that is trying to be filled. To be the one with power is to need the other side less. The one who needs less will be able to have more bargaining power through walking away and feeling indifferent towards the deal being made.

Move: The less needy you appear, the more powerful you become. Approach the other side with reluctance instead of enthusiasm. If you are too eager to make a deal, the other side will smell need and weakness and your power will drop precipitously. You are always better to be slow and reluctant to make a deal. Needy people need to make deals fast and need to concede quickly. Powerful people have the luxury of making deals slowly and conceding slowly. When they want to go fast, you go slow. When they want to go slow, you go fast. Keep them off balance.

Example: Blatantly state that you do not need or want the deal being offered: "I want your house like I want a hole in the head!" OR "The last thing I need is another house." The more clearly stated that you do not need to make a deal, the more power you will gain by eliminating your need.

Countermove: Understand that both sides have pressure. Know that the pressure is on them just as much as on you. Typically, when the other side is trying to appear powerful through showing little need is for optics only. Truly unneedy people will avoid the bargaining table altogether, and if the other side truly had no pressure to make a deal, there would be no open dialogue. Remind the other side that since you are talking there must a need because no one wants to waste time, effort, energy, or money to negotiate on something of no value. If they are spending the effort, energy, and time to come to the bargaining table, there certainly is a need. They may conceal their buying or selling pressure, but know that something motivated them to bargain with you in the first place. Find that motivation and exploit it to your advantage.

Law 24: Even Barbarians Think They Are Reasonable

Practical Gambit: The Low and Flexible Offer

No matter how savage, no matter how unruly, all human beings believe that we are reasonable. After slaughtering Prince Darius's army, Alexander the Great kept Darius's wife and family in great care. The compassion and protection he extended to Darius's family was a projection of how he would want his own family to be treated should the tables be turned. Inside of every unreasonable human being is a desire to be reasonable, no matter how crazy, savage, or barbaric they are.

Practical Gambit: The Low and Flexible Offer

Move: Making your first offer very low but indicating that you are "flexible" is a barbaric yet reasonable approach to opening a negotiation. The other side may be insulted by your extreme position, but reminding them that you are reasonable will keep them at the negotiating table long enough for them to counter. Everyone believes that they are reasonable, and flexibility is a vague term. How flexible are you? No one knows unless you are challenged.

Example: When purchasing a house at a discount say, "I know you are asking $100,000 for the house, and I'm prepared to pay $60,000 cash today, but I can be flexible if I bring the inspector and find out that your house is in great shape!" The idea of you being flexible under a certain condition gives the other side hope and a reason to keep talking. If you were to just lowball the other side without being flexible, you may have created a deadlock in the process.

Countermove: If the other side is offering you a low but flexible offer, you might as well counter them with a high and flexible offer. Nothing is more powerful than challenging all points to find the real issues. Remember both sides have buying and selling pressure, so if you challenge all points, there will be flexibility somewhere for give and take.

Law 25: There Is No Such Thing as Equal—Only Different

Practical Gambit: Splitting the Difference

In the twentieth century, humanity experimented with a concept called Communism in which all men were to be treated equal in society. They were to have equal amounts of money, equal amounts of food, and the state owned almost all property so because everyone owned nothing; all men were equal. The experiment failed because although the state forced all men into equal poverty, human beings by nature are unequal. Certain people are taller, better looking, smarter, have nicer smiles, are more charming, and so on, and no two men are equal. What remains true throughout history is that while men are not equal, they are certainly different and embracing differences and finding complementary traits is a much more productive exercise than creating a false equality.

In the twenty-first century we are trying to create a false sense of equality once again. Although the Western world is not communist, we are approaching a time where people are led to believe that we are falsely equal once more. We are not equal, and we never will be equal, only different. Although we have a deep desire to be equal and feel the justice of being the same, equality for human beings does not exist anywhere in nature.

Practical Gambit: Splitting the Difference

Move: Most novice negotiators will propose to split the difference wherever there is a gap in your price and their price. For example, you may want to buy a house for $90,000 and they may want to sell a house for $100,000. There is a $10,000 difference and most poor negotiators will propose to split the difference at $95,000. This is a bad practice, a bad habit, and an artificial expectation brought upon us by a society that raises us to believe that we are all equal. We are not equal in any way, and the difference should not be split equally. In fact, never split the difference yourself, but encourage the other side to split the difference in your favor.

Example: To split the difference in your favor, move the goal posts in your direction and manipulate the difference being split. Say: "We are $10,000 apart, why don't we split the difference? I'm at $90,000, you're at $100,000 … $99,000? $98,000? $97,000? $96,000? …" Keep suggesting that they are at lower and lower numbers until they pick their new position. They may say "We will come down to $98,000 and we'll split the difference" which would make a settling price of $94,000, which is $1,000 less than the original $95,000 "split the difference" number.

Countermove: When the other side tries to move the difference in their favor, always move the difference in your favor. You can reinforce your position by giving smaller and smaller concessions to make the other side spend more and more energy to get less and less.

Law #26: We Don't Know Our Own Minds and Neither Do They

Practical Gambit: Stick To The Main Issues

The human mind is more powerful than anything we can imagine. We may never know it's full potential. Studies say we use less than 10% of our brain on a daily basis, which leaves a vast amount of potential for emotion and thought whether conscious or subconscious. A disciplined negotiator will do his best to know himself before entering a negotiation, but in the end, the human mind is so powerful we don't know our own mind and neither does the other side. We think we know what we want, we may say we know what we want, we might even write it down, but in the heat of the moment with emotions and egos flaring and both sides with much to gain or lose, the darkness of the mind can take over and you may find yourself dramatically changing positions mid way through the negotiation. We only think we know what we want and that is simply the best we can do. Like a dog chasing a car, the dog may catch the car, but then what? The dog wanted the car, he has caught it, and now he doesn't know what to do with it. Years ago I set the goal of becoming a professional jazz musician and a professional I became. I ended up hating my life because it was what I thought I wanted, I didn't know my own mind. The first negotiation we must win is always the negotiation with ourselves; once we master ourselves can we negotiate against a live opponent.

You may have gone to the grocery store on the way home to pick up a bag of apples after work and walked out 30 minutes later with $125 of junk food even though you are on a diet. It happens everyday to someone. You may have walked into the car dealership to buy something sensible for your new family like a minivan and walk out with a hot red new sportscar. This is a frequent occurance at car dealerships. You may walk into the time-share presentation with your spouse and swear to eachother that you won't buy anything and that you are only there for the free food and show tickets and walk out with a $50,000 timeshare purchase. Every couple says this before walking into any timeshare presentation, but timeshares sales continue to be made every day. You may walk into a competing company to buy their company and when they demand an inflated price, you sell them yours instead at an equally inflated price – and they buy yours! It's more common than you think. A woman may meet a man she can't stand being around and six months later be married and madly in love with him. Retirement homes are full of old couples where the woman initially did not like the man. These are all human examples of not knowing our own minds. They seem crazy and irrational because they are and that is how the human mind works. Even the smartest, most diligent, most disciplined people succumb to this weakness in daily life because it is part of the human condition.

Your own mind will wander during the negotiation and so will theirs. To make matters worse, the other side may raise unimportant issues or make you emotional to take your focus off of the main points. Avoid this temptation, delay gratification and stick to the main issues at hand.

Move: Keep focused on the one item you want in the negotiation and avoid the emotions and clutter. Have your desired outcome written down and in front of you in your black book. When you sense that the negotiation is going off track, blatantly raise the main issues and keep them out front and center.

Example: Earlier this year I got a call from Hilton Hotels offering me four free nights in a 5-star suite if I would attend a "short" timeshare presentation is Las Vegas. A free trip sounded good to me so I took my girlfriend at the time on a short 4-day vacation and of course we attended the manditotry time-share sales presentation. The sales presenter was approachable, he was in his mid fifties, an easygoing guy and presented like he was just a normal guy "just like you". They had a great product, beautiful food offered and when the dollars and cents were calculated infront of our eyes it made rational sense to invest $25,000 in a timeshare to save $670,000 in lifetime travel costs for the next 50 years. I told my girlfriend prior to the presentation that my family already owns a timeshare that no one uses and that we were not going to buy anything.

Of course the sales presenter finishes his one and a half hour presentation of and then asks if we would like to buy. Of course I told him that I liked his product, his presentation was beautiful and it made sense but I already owned a time-share and didn't need two.

"No problem" he said as he got up to get "the closer". Lance, the closer came out of the back, he was 6'4 and built like a muscular hockey player, very smooth, tanned and blonde and the presenter and the closer sat us down for 30 minutes and attempted to negotiate a deal.

My main issue was "I already own a time share, I don't need two" and their argument was "is it really yours? Or is it your family's?" For 30 minutes we negotiated back and forth, free show tickets were thrown in valued at $300, of course when you bought a $25,000 timeshare through Hilton they convert your real dollars into "points" aka funny money and Lance started to throw in extra "points" for signing today equal to triple the value of the time share. Then the financing came out, for $1,000 down and $200 a month it can be yours today (the real price of financing was not revealed in the presentation, only funny money). Finally Lance went in for the close with "$1,000 down" he said "we could get you started today with all of these bonuses, if you were going to do this, how would you make that payment?"

My heart started to beat, he hooked my ego, of course I could pay $1,000 and I wanted to be macho and said "Visa". Realizing I was off the main issues and was becoming distracted by my own ego and ability to pay. I had to mentally backtrack to the main issue "I already own a timeshare".

The pressure was mounting. My girlfriend was nervous and the type of person who would give into such pressure, she was a "nice" girl and was studying to be an elementary school teacher. The closing team ran us through 7 attempts to close and I kept sticking to the main issue "I already have a time share we don't use" and the bonuses kept on appearing magically. Finally, Lance realized that I was sticking to my main issue, closed his sales binder and said, "Let me know if there is anything I can do" and left.

We walked out of the presentation, 3 hours later, with a mail in coupon for $99 off a Hilton Hotel room if mailed in at a certain time on a certain date, I lost the coupon and we didn't receive any of the fantastic bonuses that I wanted, but I stuck to the main issues and avoided owning two vacant time shares. My girlfriend said, "I wanted to buy, the salesman reminded me of my dad and he has to feed his family". She was ready to buy on the emotion of pity, but I stopped her by sticking to the real issues. Thankfully we didn't buy that time-share together because the relationship fell apart a few months later.

Countermove: Make them emotional about the small points in the negotiation and make them pay for their "hot buttons". There is no such thing in life as a free lunch. Free just means included with something else. Just as they may use bonuses, incentives, free lunches, rides in private planes, to woo you to making the wrong deal, you can just as easily distract them with emotional incentives of your own.

Law #27: See The Forest from the Trees

Practical Gambit: Maintain Perspective

Sometimes you will win the battle but lose the war. The phrase "winning the battle but losing the war" comes from King Pyrrhus of Epirus who defeated the Romans twice in the Pyrrhic War in 280 BC at Heracles and 279 BC at Asculum. Although King Pyrrhus defeated the Romans in battle, he could hardly enjoy his victory because he lost all of his friends and principle commanders in the fighting and could not raise new recruits to replace his lost soldiers. On the other side, the Romans were able to raise fresh soldiers just as fresh water flows out of a fountain who were not fazed by the losses of men, but in fact angered and full of sustaining force to go on with the war.

Sometimes when negotiating, we can lose perspective and fail to see the forest from the trees. We may fix on a particular item such as price and force ourselves into a deadlock. Often times when we fixate on one item and become one dimensional in negotiation, we can lose perspective all together and give away a deal that could have been won had we focused on the bigger picture.

It is always better to focus on the whole pie rather than fixating on a small slice of the same pie. The first commandment of negotiation is get what you want and get out.

Practical Gambit: Maintain Perspective

Sometimes the hardest thing when negotiating is to maintain perspective. When flying an airplane over the ocean, the pilot can get turned upside down and because the ocean and the sky are both blue, the pilot may pull "up" while turned upside down. Since the pilot has lost perspective on where the sky is relative to the ocean, when he pulled "up," his "up" is directly into the ocean—crashing the plane and killing the pilot. The same works for negotiation; if you lose your perspective on the big picture or what you truly want, you can throw it all away. Consider the man who eats a cheap cheeseburger right before he goes out to a beautiful filet mignon dinner. His appetite is spoiled on the cheap meat, and he cannot enjoy the first-class dinner he is about to have.

Move: Avoid getting sucked into the small points of a negotiation by writing down what you truly want before you begin negotiating. By writing down your desired outcome and walk-away point you can maintain perspective by the power of the written word. It's also effective to bring an unemotional partner to the bargaining table to make sure you stick to your intended outcome. In the heat of the moment, ask yourself: "If I did this deal today, how will this look a year from now"?

Example: A man and his wife have been searching for the perfect dream home. They find the perfect home, 2,000 square feet, three bedrooms, two bathrooms, a double car garage, backing onto a park and walking distance to their children's school. The house is beautiful and everything is perfect, including the price. It's July, the family can move in by August just in time for the new school year that starts in September. The man and his wife know that the asking price is $400,000 for the perfect house, so they offer $375,000. After some heavy bargaining, both parties have reached a deadlock. The seller is firm at $393,000 and the buyers are firm at $390,000—a mere $3,000 difference. At the current mortgage rates, a $3,000 difference works out to $0.42 per day but the buying couple has lost perspective and walks away from the deal. Instead they continue to live in their current home, which is much further from the children's school, not as nice, but they don't have to pay the extra $3,000. In actual fact, the costs of driving the kids to school rather than walking works out to much more than $0.42 per day, and the family is not as happy in their current home that only has two bedrooms and is much too small. They have the money to purchase the right home, but the miserly mentality of the buyers and the $3,000 difference killed the deal.

Countermove: Become the puppet master and control the other side's attention. Get them fixated on the small picture if it suits you, or get them fixated on the big picture if it suits you. Where focus goes, energy flows. You can manipulate the lens of their focus by fixating on the small picture or the big picture.

Law 28: The Strategic Mind Is Unpredictible

Practical Gambit: Whatever They Think You Will Do—Do the Opposite

I n the life of Julius Caesar, the great Roman conquerer, Caesar was captured by pirates in the mediterranean sea when he was young. The pirates locked Caesar up and demanded a ransom of twenty talents.

Some authorities say that the talent typically weighed about 33 kg (75 lb) varying from 20 to 40 kg. In February, 2016, the international price of gold was about US$1190 per troy ounce. One gram costs about $38. At this price, a talent (33 kg) would be worth about $1.25 million. So 20 talents would be $25,000,000 in today's money.

When Caesar heard that his ransom was 20 talents, he laughed and told them that they did not know who they had captured. He volunteered to pay 50 talents instead (today's value of $62,500,000). The pirates marvelled at Caesar's boldness and suddenly the tables had turned. When the pirates tried to sleep, Caesar sang to them loudly and obnoxiously to keep them awake. He wrote poetry for them and drew pictures, and when they did not admire his work, he scolded them. He roamed freely with them and participated in their games not as their captive, but as their leader. Finally, the ransom money arrived to pay off the pirates, and they let Caesar go. As soon as Caesar returned to civilization, he organized a group of soldiers and sailed back to the pirates who were counting their money. He then threw the pirates in prison and later crucified them as he said he would do in captivity. The pirates thought he was joking.

In any negotiation, to be unpredictable is to be strategic. Be bold, be un-predictable, and give them something they would never expect. To be unpredictible, imagine what the other side thinks you would do, and do they opposite. If they think that you will be soft, be firm. If they think you will go fast, go slow. If they think you are interested, become disin-terested. Nothing throws the other side off their game more then defy-ing predictability. Had Julius Caesar not demanded more than double his ransom, he may have been tortured and treated like a slave. Caesar's boldness threw the pirates off balance, and because he positioned himself as unafraid and more powerful than the pirates, he was able to control them and later destroy them.

Practical Gambit: Whatever They Think You Will Do—Do the Opposite

It is ironic to write a paragraph about becoming unpredictible because to predict unpredicitiblty is impossible. A very simple rule you can use to become unpredictible is to simply do the opposite of what the other side believes you will do. The more defiant you are of the other side, the more you will vex and confuse them. Sometimes the crazier your demands are, the more believable they are.

Example: A friend of mine went to the Apple store to purchase a brand new iPad for his assistant. Being a savvy shopper, he decided he would buy two or three iPads for the office and demand a bulk discount. Most merchants and stores will offer a bulk discount or bundle discount for two or more items. He asked the salesgirl, "Can I have a bulk discount if I buy two or three iPads? How much of a discount would I get?" The sales-girl then went to the back of the store and disappeared for some time. After many minutes she came back and said, "The bulk discount starts at 5,000 units sir, and we can only give you a very small discount." My friend was stunned by this unpredictible reply. He was predicting 10 percent or 20 percent off for buying two or three units—not 5,000 units. Only Apple as the most powerful brand in the world could set their bulk discount so high for a retail consumer good at 5,000 units. There are virtually no buyers who will order 5,000 units, so Apple will never give a discount, and that is part of their brand.

Move: Make unpredictible demands and assumptions when negotiating to throw the other side off balance. This can be risky and can potentially backfire if they don't take your bait but can be extremely powerful if you have the confidence to stand by your demands.

Countermove: Do not succumb to anything crazy. If the other side is becoming unpredictible, challenge their position and test them for validity. In all likeliness they have nothing to justify their unpredictibilty. Once you have broken their credibiltiy, force them into your status quo. Alternatively, if someone is being unpredictible with you and you cannot break them, you can be unpredictible in return. Meet their defiance with more defiance.

Law 29: Appeal to the Crocodile Brain— The Decision-Making Brain

Practical Gambit: Exploit the Power of New

The decision-making brain—the crocodile brain—is the most powerful part of our brain when it comes to making decisions. This reptilian brain only understands a very limited scope of emotions, mainly fear and greed, and has a few mechanisms built in for our survival. One mechanism is the ability to see new things in our enviornment. From mankind's early days, we lived in the jungle and had to survive off the land. Since we had to survive in a hostile enviornment, we have a section of our brain dedicated to recognizing new threats or opportunities around us to maintain our survival.

Practical Gambit: Exploit the Power of New

One of the most powerful marketing words is "new." The crocodile brain of humanity is constantly searching for new, even though there is nothing new under the sun. When negotiating, if you reach a deadlock, approach the other side with a "new" proposal. Companies are often taking old products and rebranding them as "new and improved" to capture the crocodiles in the market (which is everybody). The word "new" is so powerful that it will never go out of style because it is entrenched in the hardware of our primitive crocodile brains. This is our decision-making brain and a very powerful feature for influence.

Move: After a deadlock, approach the other side with a "new" proposal. "New" doesn't have to be that different; in fact, in can be mostly the same, but because it's "new," people will often revisit something old just to see what's "new." Ironicaly, a fairly common greeting in the English language is "what's new?" The crocodile brain is endlessly curious to hear about "new" things whether they are new or not.

Example: Every year car companies come out with a "new" version of the same old car. The car is the same under the hood; in fact, it even looks the same most times. But because it's the "new" model, it comes out at a new price and can be sold for full price. Consequently, the "old" models, or last year's models, are now depreciated, driving the market forward. The same happens in fashion. The "new" fashion of today's twenty-year-old is likely from twenty years ago when today's customer was just a baby. The baby can't remember what the "old" fashion was when it was born, so marketers take the fashion from twenty years ago and market it as "new" or vintage. The same happens with cars. Typically a car must be twenty years old to be a classic and appreciate in value. If something is really old, it can appear new.

Countermove: Challenge the validity of new. There really is nothing new under the sun, just the same old ideas shuffled around and presented in different ways.

Law 30: Force A Decision With An Ultimatum

Practical Gambit: Take It Or Leave It

ul·ti·ma·tum

əltə mādəm/

noun: ultimatum; plural noun: ultimata; plural noun: ultimatums

a final demand or statement of terms, the rejection of which will result in retaliation or a breakdown in relations.

synonyms: final offer, final demand, take-it-or-leave-it deal; threat

Origin: mid 18th century: from Latin, neuter past participle of ultimare 'come to an end.'

Forcing a decision is fittingly the last and final law and in my experience ultimatums do not work well when dealing with people in general. An ultimatum is like a loaded pistol and should only be used as a last resort. Giving an ultimatum is like the "all in" hand in poker where all of your chips are on the table and you either win it all or lose it all. Since human beings like to feel free and have the ability to make their own choices, ultimatums are very inflammatory to the ego of the otherside and will either submit them to your demands perhaps creating resentment. If they fail to take your ultimatum, your credibility will be completely destroyed and your future position at the bargaining table will

191

be severely weakened when you have to come back begging.

Everyone knows a parent who uses strict ultimatums on their children, the parent makes a "take it or leave it offer" perhaps with a consequence, the child defys, the parent loses credibilty and the relationship becomes a downward spiral of empty threats, loss of respect and zero credibility. These poor children become problem children and the parents become problem parents and eventually the child ends up in major trouble with authority in general and grows up to be a prison inmate.

Ultimatums or the "take it or leave it offer" usually works if you know that you have much more power over the other side and the power is real. With a large disparity in power ultimatums do work, but only for so long. For example if you own the "one of a kind" piece of art with high demand you can use an ultimatum, or if you are the only house for sale on a very desireable street that never sells publicly, but typically such real power is scarce. If you are the one specialist who deals with one very specific problem you can give ultimatums on your pricing because you are the one solution and very powerful, but if you have competition, you likely can't bargain this way.

Alexander the Great was able to amass an empire that covered the entire known globe at the time because he understood that when conquering people you need to either 1) befriend them and bring them into your tribe or 2) wipe them out entirely. Since genocide of entire cities and people would be too costly for him, Alexander would often leave most of the standing government intact and would win the favour of his people by good treatment, rather than by threats and ultimatums. People need to be treated well to get them to do what you want. Even after rebellions Alexander would be merciful with the defiant people, kill a few of the dissenter's leaders, put his own leaders into play and then sometimes reward and treat the rebels better than before. Although Alexander was the most powerful man in the world at the time, he also knew that being hard and giving ultimatums to his subjects would overthrow him in an instant and this was his political genius.

There is a time when ultimatums should be used and that is when all other options have been explored and you no longer wish to waste any time in the negotiation. A clear "yes" or "no" from a firm offer is better than wasting days, months or even years on a deal that is dragging on sideways and seeming to go no where. In that case, ultimatums make sense and will save you time and money. In almost every other case though, I believe that ultimatums should be used sparingly, as a final gambit and only if you are prepared to lose the relationship and the opportunity in full.

Move: You make an inflexible, final offer "take it or leave it". This will force the otherside to make a decision and either accepts your offer or decline and risk losing the relationship. This is adversarial, competitive and direct win-lose negotiation. Use with extreme caution.

Example: I used to work in a private equity company that would raise money from private investors for apartment blocks sized $5,000,000 to $25,000,000 and other business ventures. The process to sell these investments started with calling leads who showed interest, booking a first meeting at the office for a 3 hour presentation in which I knew that 30% of the time would result in a closed sale or a successful negotiation. 40% of my meetings were closed on the second meeting and the remaining 30% were closed on the third meeting. I kept statistics, as a good negotiator should to see where I was having success. If I did not make a deal on the first meeting it wasn't a problem, just part of the game, I would book a second meeting and a continuation and have a higher chance of closing. However, if I didn't close on the second meeting I would reluctantly say "Mr. Prospect, typically most people have made a decision by now on deals like this, if I book a third meeting with you, will it be a waste of time?" I would wait for his reply and then say "Ok, I will reluctantly book a third meeting, but just so you know, I never book a fourth meeting, so if you haven't made a decision by the end of the third meeting, this just isn't for you." Forcing a decision by me telling the prospect up front held great power for me because it either got them "in or out" so I could focus my time on making more deals. As a salesperson my offer was inflexible in that I had no "wiggle room" so it was indeed a "take it or leave it," offer.

Countermove: Take it or leave it is a maximum power play and to defy maximum power you use maximum defiance. Simply walk away from the deal if you can afford to and let them approach you. This is a game of chicken and whoever gives in first loses major power by crawling back.

Very often you see bad negotiators use "take it or leave it" too early or too often and simply defying them will counter this technique instantly. It takes virtually no skill to counter, "take it or leave it", just walk away and let them chase you.

Part V:

How To Negotiate By Reading Body Language

How To Negotiate By Reading Body Language

Initially I did not intend to include information on body language in this book about negotiating because I believed that a book was the wrong way to show body language. Why tell when you can show? But upon further consideration, I believe that a field manual with general guidelines for reading body language and learning the fundamentals would be invaluable to any negotiator especially when paired with pictures in illustrated form.

The following body language study was learned by an ex FBI agent named Joe Navarro. Joe's training has been invaluable to me and has helped me navigate through the many negotiations found in business and in life.

Body Language Fundamentals

Body language is so important to your ability to negotiate because:

- 58 percent of communication is body language.

- 3 percent of communication is tone.

- 8 percent of communication is words.

The other day I was watching a coworker of mine say "yes" with his words while shaking his head "no." I wondered if my coworker was aware that his body language said "no" even though he was trying to say "yes." Unfortunately, our lives in personal and business are littered with strange conflicting communications like the one I just described. To truly understand what someone is saying to you, you must read beneath their words and tone and into their body language.

Unfortunately, there is no way to use body language to tell if someone is lying or not. Studies have concluded that there is no definitive way to tell if someone is lying or not from body language alone; however, what is certainly detected through body language is one of two things: comfort or discomfort.

If body language was to be summed up in one sentence it would be:

All body language is a communication of comfort or discomfort.

There is no way to tell if someone is lying or telling the truth, but you can certainly tell if they are becoming more or less comfortable, which can give you clues into deeper meanings.

The Three Human Brains and Body Language

To continue our study into the three human brains—the reptilian brain, the mammalian brain and the thinking brain—body language is extremely connected to these three brains in many ways. Typically, we will be dealing with the reptilian brain, which handles the bodily functions. Often, the neocortex or the thinking brain will be trying to think and be calm, while the reptilian brain is making the body fidget. Understand that body language is a calamity of these three brains trying to work together, and to review:

- The reptilian brain—handles body function, breathing, blinking, fidgeting, etc.

- The mammalian brain—controls our fight or flight/flock/freeze instincts and our emotions

- The upper brain (neocortex)—in charge of our thinking, logic, creativity, and words. It also gives us the ability to fabricate, lie, cheat, and steal.

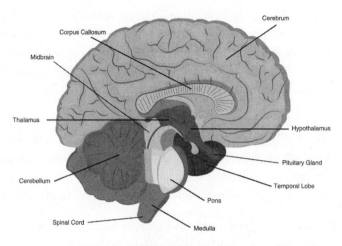

Pacificers

When a person is uncomfortable, he or she will "pacify" and soothe themselves like a mother stroking a baby to calm the baby down. Except we are the baby and mommy isn't around, so instead we soothe ourselves to create comfort in uncomfortable situations. Sometimes soothing can be to create comfort, enhance comfort, or mask discomfort. We can see soothing happening through twirling hair, scratching skin, curling toes, moving fingers, playing with a pen or pencil, tapping toes, or other fidgeting. A person who is soothing is trying to become more comfortable and the question is, what is making him uncomfortable? It's your job to find out.

Ten Rules of Body Language

1.) Become a competent observer, always look for clues—much like listening is more important than talking in negotiation, watching and observing is more important when reading body language than anything else. Train yourself to watch and observe; look for fine details and small body movements. Are you observing comfort or discomfort?

2.) Nonverbal cues belong in context to show what's going on in a person's life—Do the nonverbal cues make sense in the context you are observing? Is the man touching his nose because he is cold or because he's uncomfortable? Those two actions may look the same, but depending on the context, they may mean different things.

3.) Differentiate between limbic behavior and cultural—limbic behaviors are controlled by the reptilian brain and are automatic, as in they happen without thinking. Cultural behaviors can be the same. You must learn to differentiate between cultural movements and limbic movements. Both are automatic, and your prospect doesn't have to think to execute them.

4.) Is this behavior specific to this individual? Most people have specific repeated behaviors. Everyone has their quirks; is this individual performing that behavior because it is a quirk? Or is it a sign of discomfort?

5.) Nonverbal communication needs to be examined in clusters, not one dimensionally. It is nearly impossible to take one piece of nonverbal behavior and assess it alone. To get an accurate read on body language you must read a cluster of behaviors to get a clear picture.

6.) Ask, what is normal behavior for this person in this situation? Does the behavior make sense?

7.) Ask, what behaviors are a change from normal?

8.) Focus on primacy. For example, the first expression someone gives you is likely the most accurate to their feelings because the limbic brain reacts first. The thinking brain may force different body language if they have time to think.

9.) Observations we make are nonintrusive. Do not inquire or intrude into a person while observing, or you will alter their behavior.

10.) If unsure of what behavior means, classify it as comfort or discomfort. This is the most important part of reading body language.

Feet Don't Lie

Feet are extremely important for reading body language because we often do not think of masking our feet. The limbic brain will react, and we may be culturally trained to control our faces, but not our feet. In addition, as readers of body language, we typically read faces, heads, and hands. However, the feet show comfort or discomfort just as easily as other body parts. Comfort shows the feet moving together as if to relax and discomfort shows the feet moving apart to fight or run.

If you are at a restaurant, you can see which couples are in love by their feet touching. You can also see which couples are having problems by having their feet far apart. The same applies in bed with lovers; if the feet are touching, it's a sign of love.

Years ago when I used to ride the bus, I would observe the feet of the other people at the bus stop. In a group of people, a person will point their feet towards the person they find the most attractive. When I noticed someone had their feet pointing towards me, I would engage them in friendly conversation. If their feet were turned away, I would avoid engaging them.

Legs

Legs are an extension of the feet and also something that we are not taught to mask our feelings with. Thus, legs are very accurate indicators

of how we feel.

Crossed legs are an indication of comfort. When legs are crossed, a person's balance will be tipped toward a person they favor.

When strangers are present, this will cause the legs to uncross and the feet to plant on the floor as if to run.

In contrast to the comfortable leg cross, is the uncomfortable leg cross, which has one leg over top to act as a barrier. This would be to kick an offender and then run. Whenever someone is placing a barrier like a leg between you and them, it's a sign of discomfort.

As a transition, we may initially have our legs crossed in comfort and should we be discomforted by something, we may switch to the defensive leg cross, which would make us ready to subconsciously create a barrier, "kick" and run.

Two people who are in rapport will walk at synchronized walking speeds, and their legs will move together. In contrast, two people out of synch shows a disharmony between the pair. Typically when walking, we adjust our speed to the person of higher status, it's automatic.

Stance

Use of space and how we command our space shows how confident we are in our situation. Typically men try to become bigger and take up more room while women try to take up less room. When commanding your space, do you own the room? Or does the room own you?

How do you feel about the idea you are selling? Your confidence will show in how much room you take up.

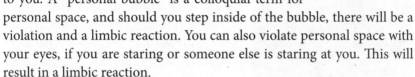

Personal Space

Every person has a different idea of what personal space means. You can typically tell the size of a person's "personal bubble" by where they stand relative to you. A "personal bubble" is a colloquial term for personal space, and should you step inside of the bubble, there will be a violation and a limbic reaction. You can also violate personal space with your eyes, if you are staring or someone else is staring at you. This will result in a limbic reaction.

Certain objects will be comfortable in a prospect's personal space, and foreign objects will create discomfort. Likewise, if a personal item is removed personal space, discomfort will be created.

Hips Don't Lie

Hips are indicators of emotion; they represent sexual reproduction, sexual health, and sexual interest in other people. Shifting of hips shows discom-

fort while sitting. Pleasing, or happy, hip movements are shown when dancing or seductive.

Hands on hips can be a sign of territory if the thumbs are concealed behind a person's back, whereas hands on hips can be a friendly gesture if the thumbs are forward and showing.

Genital framing, which is framing the hips with the hands, is a sign of sexuality and confidence.

Torso

The torso is a very important part of the body because it shows age, health, and social status. Around the world, the torso is the place used for decoration—we drape clothes, medals, awards, achievements, pins, and

jewelry on our torsos. Showing your torso is a sign of honesty. Typically, a two-button suit creates more trust than a three-button suit because it shows more of the chest, which represents vulnerability. Below is a picture of JFK and Richard Nixon at a key historic presidential debate. The debate is historic because it was the first time that Americans could watch the debate on TV and hear at the same time what the hopeful presidents were saying. Previous to this point in history, all Americans had to listen to the debates on the radio. In this presidential debate between JFK and Nixon, the people who listened to the debate on the radio thought that Nixon won because of his superior verbiage and speaking skills, but JFK ended up winning overall because his body language, health, suit, posture, and grooming were all superior to Nixon.

Crossing of Arms

Crossing of arms is typically a mechanism to create a barrier between

one person and another. Barriers are indicators of discomfort. However, you need to distinguish between crossed arms for comfort and crossed arms for discomfort. The difference lies in the grip of the hands. A soft grip vs a tight grip will show the difference between comfort and discomfort.

Ventral Fronting/Ventral Denial

ven·tral

ventr l/

adjective ANATOMYZOOLOGYBOTANY

adjective: ventral

of, on, or relating to the underside of an animal or plant; abdominal. "a ventral nerve cord"

Ventral means the soft side of an animal or plant. In the case of most animals, including humans, the ventral side is soft and unarmored and has lots of delicate veins responsible for keeping the animal alive. With most animals, showing the ventral side of the body is exposing vulnerability and by contrast, showing the dorsal side is to create protection and hide vulnerability.

dor·sal

dôrs l/

adjective ANATOMYZOOLOGYBOTANY

adjective: dorsal

of, on, or relating to the upper side or back of an animal, plant, or organ. "a dorsal view of the body"

Neck and Head

In most body language, we move towards things that we like and move away from things we don't like. Neck tilting is usually a sign of comfort or liking someone. Discomfort with the neck and head would show a stiffening of the neck and the head will stand up straight as if to look, listen, and perhaps run.

Hands and Arms

Hands and arms show comfort or discomfort by exposing the ventral or dorsal side. Arms are easily used for protection and to create barriers, or they can easily be used to show vulnerability by displaying the wrists and the palms. Hands and arms are used as protective barriers because if an animal were to attack your arm, you would live, but if the same animal attacked the ventral side of your chest or neck, you may not live. The hands and arms are thus used to protect the chest and neck.

Preening

Preening is a sign of respect or disrespect depending on the context. When an important person walks into a room, the respectful gesture is to quickly adjust the hair, glasses, jewelry or ties and stand up before greeting them.

A sign of disrespect while preening is to do it while others are talking. You can see this behavior with criminals challenging authority or teenagers challenging authority.

Handshake Dos and Don't

Handshake delivery is specific to different cultures. In a construction culture, there is a very firm grip, almost to the point of pain. When shaking someone else's hand, you will see how they learned how to shake hands. There is no universal handshake that works across every group of people or every culture. It's best to mimic what the other person is doing to you, and I prefer to be slightly firmer than them.

Handshakes can be twisted for dominance or submission. A submissive handshake will have the wrist facing up and the palm open. A dominant handshake will have the wrist facing down, the dorsal side facing up.

Sometimes in a handshake, one hand will try to twist the other to get the dominant position. This is apparent with world leaders and politicians when they meet on the international stage and want to show dominance to the world.

When two world leaders will shake, one will gain the other hand, the other will twist wrists to gain the advantage, and then the loser will touch the winner on the elbow with his free hand, and the winner will touch the elbow of the loser.

Do not do the two-handed handshake, which has been studied across cultures and is never viewed as favorable.

The Face as a Canvas

From birth we are taught to read faces. As babies we look up to our mothers and read their expressions. From all of this practice, the face is one of the easiest places to see emotion. We are also excellent at reading facial emotion because we practice the most on the face.

We may be good at concealing our facial expressions from time to time, but the one part of the face that is very hard to conceal is the forehead. We often don't think about concealing our foreheads, so emotion shows easily there.

Eyes are the windows to the soul, and concealing the eyes is a blocking mechanism. Wearing sunglasses is a way to have your eyes become unreadable. If you watch world class poker tournaments, you will see professional poker players wearing sunglasses and cowboy hats to conceal their foreheads and eyes.

Dilated pupils indicate something we like to see as if we want it to come

towards us. Constricted pupils show discomfort and are immediately focused on distance and a threat further away.

Smile with the Eyes

A true smile is a smile done with the eyes. A fake smile is done with the mouth only while the eyes show some other emotion. Around the eyes you will also see wrinkles on older people which will show you optimism if the crow's feet point up, pessimism if they point down and neutrali-

ty if they are straight across. The wrinkles around the eyes and the forehead will show a lifetime of smiles or a lifetime of hardship.

The Nose Knows

The nose can be a place to pacify discomfort. Touching the nose has to be taken in context. A person touching their nose while standing in line, writing an exam, or waiting, for example, will give far less information than a person pacifying by touching their nose in a tough situation. There is no scientific way to see if a person is lying or not from body language, although some people think that touching of the nose indicates lying.

Dilated nostrils indicate that the prospect is about to do something physical, like hit you. Think about an enraged bull about to charge: his nostrils flare, and then he attacks. The same is true with people.

Licking of lips is another form of pacifying. Watch for other subtle cues of pacifying.

Disappearing Lips

When lips disappear it's a sign of high stress. Pursed lips show a sign of disagreement. If you are negotiating with someone and they purse their lips after you make a statement it means that they disagree with you.

Chin Touching versus Pacifying

Touching the chin can mean two very different things. A narrow chin touch shows that the prospect is thinking, but a wide chin touch is an indicator of pacifying.

Part VI:
Eight Elements of Power and How to Increase Your Personal Power

Eight Elements of Power and How to Increase Your Personal Power

"No man is wise enough, nor good enough to be trusted with unlimited power."

—Charles Colton

Power and the study of power has fascinated people for centuries. Power is seen and used in politics, in business, in love, and in war, and seemingly in every human interaction there is some element of power being used. Power is simply defined as the ability to get things done. Whether it be move an object across a room, influence an audience, start or stop a war, power is needed. The value of power is so fundamental to human beings that it is indeed a fundamental value and need for every person. We must have a certain amount of power to be happy and get things done in life.

In negotiating, knowing how and when to use power is a way to create leverage and a stronger position. The eight elements of power that are shared in this book are for positing purposes and can be stacked upon on another. You can use one type of power to gain advantage or use multiple elements of power at once for greater effect. The elements of power that we will explore in this section are:

Element #1: Power of Legitimacy

Element #2: Power of Prizes

Element #3: Power of Punishment

Element #4: Power of Integrity

Element #5: Power of Charisma

Element #6: Power of Expertise

Element #7: Power of Timing

Element #8: Power of Information

Some readers may feel negative about power as if power is about manipulating or harming people. When reading this section, understand that power is neutral; it is neither good nor bad and can be used for either good or evil. Power is a tool and will be used as the wielders of power see fit. Consider the atomic bomb that was dropped on Japan at the end of World War II. Some would argue that the power of that bomb was horrible and killed and maimed many people along with destroying great Japanese cities at the time. The other side of the argument is that the power of the atomic bomb saved lives because it stopped a war that was dragging on too long, and many more people would have died through prolonged fighting. Regardless of your opinion on which side is right and which side is wrong, we can surely agree that such a bomb is powerful and can be used in a negative way to kill and destroy or in a positive way to prevent further wars.

Element #1: Power of Legitimacy

The first element of power that must be learned is the power of legitimacy. As human beings we succumb to the "aura of legitimacy" portrayed by others in negotiations. If we see a person with the title of "vice president" we assume that he is important. If we see an official looking price tag at the jewelry store we believe that the price is real. Titles, the written word, and other trappings like business cards, brands, logos, and imagery all make up an "aura of legitimacy" that lend power to the person who appears to be legitimate.

Consider a medical doctor. When your medical doctor steps into his office and you have been waiting on the paper-covered examining table after the nurse took your blood pressure and checked your heart rate and weight, the legitimacy of someone who is called a doctor, wearing a white coat and looks the part creates an "aura of legitimacy" that makes us listen to whatever the doctor prescribes. The doctor will write us an official prescription on an official piece of doctor paper, and we accept any drug he prescribes because he is indeed a doctor. We do not consider the fact that the drug the doctor is prescribing is from a company he owns shares in, or the fact that the doctor may not actually know what is wrong with you. The fact is, the doctor is a doctor, he has a title, appears legitimate, and we accept his word as true. That is the power of legitimacy.

The power of legitimacy extends to presidents or anyone else of power. The president of the United States would be expected to ride in a limo, not a Honda civic. He would be expected to have one of his staff carry his luggage up the steps into the White House and not carry it himself. If the president does not look and act like a president, he loses his power of legitimacy, and the people stop believing in him.

For you to have the power of legitimacy, you must use your title or create one if you do not have one yet. In my real estate office, the entry level job for real estate is the "Vice President of Acquisitions." In reality, this job is entry level and anyone can be the "vice president," but when people in the industry get a call from the "vice president of acquisitions" they are more likely to talk to the legitimate-sounding person on the phone, whether he has been in the business for five minutes or for five years. Of course the vice president must have the confidence to carry out his "aura of legitimacy" for his power to be maintained.

Another way to create more power is to remove your first name from your business cards and all of your communications in general. Consider many successful authors H. G. Wells, J. K. Rowling, L. R. Hubbard—anyone who uses their initials as their first name is forcing the other side to call them "Mr. Wells" or "Ms. Rowling." To remove your first name is to increase your power because it removes any chances of getting onto a first-name basis.

Another way to create power of legitimacy for yourself when negotiating is to use your office, automobile, or territory where you are surrounded by your own trappings of power. You may have your title on your desk, your awards you have won, your receptionist to make the other side wait in the lobby, the nice leather chair you sit in versus the plastic folding one that they sit in. When you control the territory, you create legitimacy for yourself. It is always more powerful to meet in your office surrounded by your trappings of power than to meet at your home or kitchen table. Real estate sales people understand the power of legitimacy and will typically lease a luxury car like a Mercedes, BMW, Porsche, Range Rover, or Lexus to create the aura of legitimacy when negotiating with clients. In reality, the salesperson may be broke and not have any money to make the payments, but it is always more powerful to negotiate in a beautiful, spotless, leather interior of a brand new Mercedes than it is to negotiate in a ten-year-old Toyota with kids' toys in the back, spilled milk on the seat, and a melted chocolate bar on interior car mat.

Another way to create the power of legitimacy is to have a secretary screen and place your calls. You may find this pretentious, but the harder you are to access, the more perceived power you have. In the insurance business, brand new agents who are male, will get a female to record their voicemail message. In reality, these sales agents are dead broke and are just starting out in the industry. They cannot afford a secretary, but the female voice on the voicemail creates the "aura of legitimacy" that creates power and prestige on the side of the new agent.

Other ways that people and companies use the power of legitimacy is through your positioning in the marketplace. You may be the:

1.) biggest

2.) smallest

3.) best

4.) worst

5.) oldest

6.) newest

7.) award winning

positioned player in the marketplace, and this adds to your power of legitimacy.

When you have the power of legitimacy, what you will earn is respect. Consider the respect for the law that everyday citizens have where you may be stuck at a red light in the middle of the night and no one is around. Rather than running the red light, most people will wait at the red light merely out of respect for the legitimate power of the law.

Tradition is another form of legitimate power. The power lies in the fact that "we have done this for a long time" and because they have done this for a long time, we assume that the tradition is legitimate. We do not question old and outdated traditions merely on the fact that they have been around so long that they have become legitimate.

With respect to legitimacy, consider the fact that in any endeavor, you will start out illegitimate and brand new, but if you survive in the endeavor long enough, you eventually become legitimate. Consider where the line between illegitimate and legitimate is. I challenge you to find it; you may find that the fact that you have "been around for a long time" suddenly makes you legit. You may know someone who has "been in the business for twenty years." They may say that to create legitimacy in their business practices, but consider the fact that they may have done the same year twenty times in a row and may not be any good at what they do. You may want someone who has been in the business for one year, but with a stellar track record.

Along with tradition are established procedures or "company policies." Many businesses use price tags, and most consumers do not question the price tag on any item. Most items are negotiable when it comes to price, but the power of legitimacy and the written word make us comply with established procedures and prices.

Standard contracts and forms are another way to create the power of legitimacy. When a consumer makes a purchase it always looks more legitimate to print a contract on three-ply charcoal paper that creates a white copy, a yellow copy, and a pink copy with full return policies and procedures on it than it would be to write the customer's credit card number down on a cocktail napkin and stuff it in your pocket. The standard contract with three copies allows the customer to take one home, the sales agent to keep one, and the company to process one copy. In reality, the contract is barely better than the napkin, but the power of legitimacy is what captures the heart and mind of the customer.

Element #2: Power of Prizes

The phrase "bread and circuses" originated in Rome by the poet Juvenal in circa 100 A.D. The phrase identifies the problem in society where the populace only cares for the prizes of "bread" (free bread from the government and politicians in power) and "circuses" (gladiator and chariot games that entertain the masses). Since the average man only cares for bread and circuses, he no longer cares for his political birthright of political involvement and who is in power. The power of prizes has taken over a once-powerful republic. Rome originated as a powerful stoic democracy where the people were involved in voting and controlling the government. The government feared the power of the people, not the other way around. When the elected politicians realized that they could buy the votes of the people with "prizes," typically, free grain, bread, and gladiator games, the political system became a race to the bottom to see who could give more prizes to the people in exchange for poorer and poorer governance. Throughout history, democracy only lasts for about 250 years until the people find out that they can vote themselves prizes and the system collapses.

"When the people find that they can vote themselves (prizes) money, that will herald the end of the republic."

—BENJAMIN FRANKLIN

Such is the power of the prize. When there is promise of a reward, people will give up their power in exchange for the prize or the reward. In Rome the people gave up their political involvement for free grain and free entertainment. Today in America, the same thing is happening; the people give up their involvement for bread and circuses, and this signals the end of the 250-year life span of democracy and the end of the republic, very much like Rome.

The ability to create a prize and reward for the other side is a tremendous source of power. In a taxi cab company, the dispatcher has more power than the owner because he can reward the cab drivers with more jobs and in effect more money. The person who can give the prizes is the person with the power.

When you are negotiating in business, you can use the power of prizes when you position yourself. You are the best in the business, and doing business with the best is a reward unto itself. There is always a market for the best and always a market for the cheapest. However, there is much more profit in being the best and positioned as the prize.

To create prize power in your business, you must put your personal reputation on the line to solve the buyer's problems. When you take on their problems, you are rewarding them; they are not rewarding you with the business. Most junior salespeople will feel like the customer is the prize and that the customer is rewarding the salesperson with the business. Professional salespeople who are the best in the business use the power of prizes to frame the situation differently. Professionals know that they are the prize and that they are rewarding the client with the best service in the industry, and that is why a great salesperson is a prize to be won by the customer.

When you utilize the power of prizes and frame yourself as the prize, you will have the confidence to ask your customer for all of their business rather than begging like a dog for a small share of the customer's table scraps. You are the prize to be won—use prize power to your advantage.

Prize power can also be used as an intimidation factor. Whenever you feel as though the other side can reward you or give you a prize, you feel the power of prizes creep in. A junior salesperson may be intimidated with the prize power of his first $1,000 sale whereas a pro salesperson won't feel any pressure with a $100,000 sale. In fact, the more you ignore the power of prizes and ability that the other side has to reward you, the greater your power will be in relation to the other side.

Prize power can also be intimidating in the sexual arena. Consider a young man who is going on a date with a very beautiful woman who is "out of his league." He may feel as though she is the prize and lose his confidence and his power when dealing with her. The same man can change his mind and tell himself that he is the prize and that she is lucky to be out with him, and there will be an entire shift of power on the date.

Other prizes that may be available for intimidation purposes may be opportunities to do business in the future, access to a ski cabin, free trips, free food, opportunities for exposure, or any other rewards that you may find attractive. Maintain your power and do not be tempted by the power of prizes.

"A nation is born a stoic and dies an epicurean."

—WILL DURANT

---

sto·ic
stōik/

noun

noun: stoic; plural noun: stoics; noun: Stoic; plural noun: Stoics

1. a person who can endure pain or hardship without showing their feelings or complaining.

Ep·i·cu·re·an
epiky rē n epi kyo orē n/

noun

noun: Epicurean; plural noun: Epicureans

1. a disciple or student of the Greek philosopher Epicurus.

a person devoted to sensual enjoyment, especially that derived from fine food and drink.

Element #3: Power of Punishment

Power of punishment is the opposite of the power of prizes. While the power of prizes alludes to the fact that the other side can reward you with intangible pleasurable benefits like money, fame, travel, love, sex, more business, or whatever else you desire, the power of punishment is the opposite of pleasure. The power of punishment is indeed the perception that the other side can punish or harm you rather than reward you.

Consider the intimidation factor of power of punishment when a police officer pulls you over on the highway and has the power to give you a speeding ticket—or not. In that situation of intimidation, the police officer has the power of punishment.

Parents with children will use the power of prizes along with the power of punishment with their children: "If you finish your vegetables you will get an extra cookie with dessert" versus "If you don't finish your vegetables, no playtime after dinner, and you go straight to bed."

Element #4: Power of Morality

The power of morality is awarded to those who have a consistent set of values and follow through on them. A person with high integrity and a set of unchanging values will always have more power than a person who changes his values frequently.

Consider the pope, the leader of the Catholic Church: although the Catholic Church has been responsible throughout history in killing, plunder, rape, murder, and theft and was responsible for one of the most terrible times in European history known as the Dark Ages, the pope, because of his unwavering values, is one of the most powerful people on the planet.

How powerful is your decision making ability? Are you a person who will stick to your decisions or go back on them? Do you take back an ex-lover or do you go crawling back when you are in a weak moment? The person who sticks to his decisions and his values will have the power of morality on his side.

Power of morality comes into play when you do what's right for the customer even if you send them to a competitor. Zappos, now a division of Amazon, is a major online shoe retailer where the sales staff is trained to find the right shoe for the customer even if they have to send the customer to a competitor. This power of morality creates massive trust between the customer and Zappos and wins loyal customers and huge sales in the long run. At Zappos they also use the power of morality when hiring staff. At the end of the two-week paid staff training, they offer a $2,000 bonus to anyone who wants to quit on the spot and not work for the company. This example of power of morality gives the bad employees a chance to save face and leave before they cost the company money by offering bad customer service or working for a company that their heart is not invested in. When you bribe bad employees to leave, this builds massive trust on the entire Zappos team and creates a very strong culture of performance.

To maintain your power of morality, avoid setting standards and then breaking your own standards. Avoid saying that you never cut prices and then cut prices. This confuses the people around you and destroys your power.

The benefit of using the power of morality versus the power of prizes is that long-lasting values have a long-term effect, whereas the power of prizes and punishment have a short-term effect. When you use the power of prizes to reward a child too often, very soon the child takes the prizes for granted and learns to expect rewards every time for the same behavior.

Building up your power of morality by having a strong set of values and sticking to them consistently brings trust and leverage into any negotiation. In fact, when negotiating against someone with strong values and high integrity, especially against cutting prices, you soon learn to not even ask for a concession. I have been an Apple Computers customer my entire life, and I used to ask for discounts on my new computer purchase every five years. Apple will always respond with "We don't discount our products" and in fact, they do not give discounts to the public ever. Apple is so strong in the power of morality and sticking to their values that even after owning a Mac computer for years, you can still sell it for almost full value years later on the secondary market. The power of morality keeps Apple's brand strong. Their products are excellent, and thus a competitor's computer will sell for pennies on the dollar years later, and the Mac computer will sell for nearly full price after years of use. Such is the power of morality and sticking to a consistent set of values.

Another trend where companies are using the power of morality to create massive trust in the marketplace is a company like Tom's Shoes who gives away a pair of shoes to a person in need for every pair that you buy. Tom's Shoes doesn't mention in their marketing that they give away so many shoes to third-world countries like Haiti that they completely destroy the local shoe makers and shoe economies; that is not part of moral power. Instead, they have a strong set of values, and this strong set of values helps Tom's Shoes become a major seller of shoes around the world, regardless of the positive and negative effects of such morality.

Moral Power as an Intimidation Tool

As human beings we marvel at people who live by a consistent set of values. To be human is to be flawed, and at some point everyone may violate his or her values.

If you find that someone is using the power of morality against you, you may neutralize their power by (1) finding a precedent where the exception beat the rule or (2) establish that the policy they are enforcing on you may have worked in the past but is no longer relevant going forward. Rules were meant to be broken, and in negotiation morals and ethics are merely weapons that one group of people will use to gain advantage over another.

Element #5: Power of Charisma

cha·ris·ma
k rizm /

noun

noun: charisma; plural noun: charismata

1. compelling attractiveness or charm that can inspire devotion in others. "she enchanted guests with her charisma"

synonyms: charm, presence, personality, force of personality, strength of character; Moremagnetism, attractiveness, appeal, allure "he lacks the charisma we look for in our salespeople"

2. a divinely conferred power or talent.

Power of charisma is hard to classify and hard to identify. Charisma is a "gift from god" or a "special talent" such as the ability to heal or prophesize. In modern terms, charisma is the ability to capture the heart and mind of another person and gain support or devotion.

Other ways to look at the power of charisma could be the power of personality, power of celebrity, or the power of being liked. We always wish to please people that we like, and the power of charisma can be completely magical. Consider the special treatment that rock stars get when they travel across the country. Celebrities get free cars, free travel, free food, and a multitude of other benefits from their power of charisma.

To be likeable and charismatic is to be powerful. People have a hard time saying no to a person they like. Consider a cute little three-year-old girl asking for a cookie. She is cute and has charisma, so you will give her the cookie.

Power Of Charisma as an Intimidation Factor

Power of charisma can be very intimidating in that we are less inclined to ask for concessions from people that we like. In fact, a charismatic negotiator can often make deals that would be impossible for an uncharismatic person to make. If you study top salespeople or negotiators you will find the power of charisma as an intangible X factor they have either developed or were born with.

Element #6: Power of Expertise

When you project more expertise on a subject than other people, you have power over them. A doctor, auto mechanic, plumber, even a maid when choosing the cleaning products for your home, or a waiter at a fancy restaurant will have power of expertise when making recommendations to you. We all want to be guided by experts, and as human beings we are trained socially to look to experts to learn what we should think about any particular subject.

Power Of Expertise as an Intimidation Factor

Do not be intimidated by someone who appears to be an expert. The expert is merely someone who is at least one step ahead of the person they are advising. Oftentimes, experts are merely people who are self-proclaimed experts and may not even have any special knowledge or expertise at all. Consider a realtor who claims to be the local area expert. What qualifies him to be the expert? The fact that he lives on a street in the neighborhood? He is merely the expert because he calls himself the expert.

Conversely, when someone questions your expertise on a matter and you may lack the expertise to maintain power, simply say "That is not my area of expertise, but my team is the finest in the business, and I have someone with that expertise on my team."

Using different and specific language is a major ploy for using the power of expertise to gain advantage over others. Doctors and lawyers will use different language on you to appear more technical and more powerful.

Instead, get them to speak in plain English to take the expertise and intimidation factor away. You can strip the power of expertise completely away from people using special language on you to get them to explain the technical jargon, using grade four language or as I like to say, "Explain that to me as if I'm a three-year-old."

Element #7: Power of Timing

The power of timing is found when people who normally don't have any power suddenly have power over you. Consider the clerk at the government office who has no power to choose how he does his job and suddenly you show up his desk and need something from him. This government worker with limited power typically will exercise all of his power over you because in this situation and this specific timing, he will have all of the power, and you have none. Generally, people with very little power love to use it when they get a chance.

You can see the power of timing with building inspectors, desk clerks, secretaries, government workers, and so on. These people have very little power in real life, but under certain timings and circumstances, their power is magnified immensely.

Element #8: Power of Information

With the proliferation of computers in the 1990s, the industrial age ended when the Berlin wall came down, and we entered the information age. The power of information is extremely valuable when negotiating because the sharing of information bonds people together. When you share information with your customers, you create value and this shared information bonds the customer to you. Pharmaceutical reps typically can only book meetings with busy doctors if they have new information about a drug or specific research. I used to work for a company in Canada that shared more free information in the marketplace than any other competitor, and in a few short years the startup company grew to a multi-million-dollar revenue company and became the fortieth fastest growing company in the country. Such is the power of information and its ability to build trust in a negotiation.

Power Of Information as an Intimidation Factor

Secrets and withheld information can be used to manipulate the confidence levels of negotiators in any negotiation. Secrets and withheld information may increase or decrease your confidence in any situation.

Stacking Power

I f you study top salespeople and top negotiators around the world, you will notice that they will use multiple types of power at once and will "stack" power for maximum leverage and advantage. A sales leader in most industries will use all eight types of power to his advantage, namely:

Power of Legitimacy—A sales leader will have a fancy title "regional vice president." He will look like a president and act like the owner of the company.

Power of Prizes—The sales leader will have some specific reward or prize for taking action today, perhaps a special discount or rebate for taking action now.

Power of Punishment—The sales leader will also have something that will be lost for those who do not take action today.

Power of Morality—The sales leader will appeal to the power of morality by serving a higher purpose or sticking to a strong set of values of doing what is right for the customer. He may even donate a percentage of his profits to charity to show morality.

Power of Charisma—The sales leader will be charismatic and well-liked by many types of people. He will typically be physically fit, well dressed, well spoken, well mannered, and have a good sense of humor with a high degree of agreeableness.

Power of Expertise—The sales leader will be framed as an expert in his field.

Power of Timing—The sales leader will have the power of timing on his side in that now is the perfect time to act on his offer

Power of Information—The sales leader will use information to his advantage and may offer you a free report, free book, or any other materials you will need to make a decision today.

Other Forms Of Power

Power of Crazy

To convince the other side that you are crazy is to have power over them. You are unpredictable and you are powerful. The power of unpredictability is terrifying to most intelligent, rational people. We like to be able to predict the outcomes of dealing with another person, and nothing is more powerful than a man with nothing to lose or everything to gain.

Power of Risk Displacement, Risk Sharing, or Risk Reversal

One way to create power in a negotiation is to give a risk reversal guarantee where the seller will offer a money-back guarantee if their product does not perform. To manipulate risk, displace it, share it, or reverse it is extremely powerful at the bargaining table. Besides reversing risk, you can also share the risk of the upside or downside of a deal. Consider a real estate syndication where instead of contributing $1,000,000 to a large real estate project, investors are much more comfortable to break the $1,000,000 into 100 x $10,000 units. Smaller risk, smaller reward, can be very powerful in this situation.

Power of Confusion

As an extension of power of information is the power of confusion. They say in sales that a confused mind does not buy. However, creating confusion by having too many moving parts or too much complexity can create power for you as a seller or a buyer. Creating confusion can create need, and need disempowers the other side and makes them more willing to buy your solution. Use confusion to your advantage by offering a confusing problem and your simple solution.

Power of Competition

The person who has more options always has more power in any negotiation. Consider the power of competition, when there are multiple buyers, say ten, fifteen, or twenty buyers for a single property. The property will enter into a bidding war where the buyers will strip their offers of conditions and escalate their buying price to irrational levels just to win. The human spirit is very competitive, and although we may not admit to loving a competition, we all love to win. Whenever you can get multiple people competing for one job or one opportunity, you will create leverage and advantage just by using the power of competition.

Final Thoughts

Thank you for taking the time to invest in yourself and increase the value of your #1 asset – you! The world needs more people like you; self-educating independent people are the future leaders of this planet. Writing this project took a lot longer than I thought, nearly two years, much more research and study than I anticipated and I hope that you were able to derive real concrete value from my work.

Negotiation is a subject that everyone needs, but no one wants to buy. It's unsexy by nature, compared to "getting rich in real estate" but you have taken the road less travelled and because so few people travel this road, you will have a tremendous advantage in the real world. I respect your time and hope that I have made the best use of it. You are Self Made, and you are on a journey, I salute you in the pursuit of your highest and greatest self.

Should you need to reach me for questions, help, speaking engagements or any other reason, please email my admin team and it will get forwarded direct to me support@stefanaarnio.com

Respect The Grind,

Stefan Aarnio

My Purpose

"Give a man a fish and he's fed for a day.

Teach a man to fish and he's fed for life.

Teach a man to teach fishermen and end world hunger!

STEFAN AARNIO'S

BLUEPRINT
TO CA$H

Stefan Aarnio's Blueprint to cash is the
perfect "next step" for anyone curious
in learning the fundamentals of buying,
fixing and selling homes for profit!

BlueprintToCash.com

For more information on Stefan Aarnio's
award winning System for finding, funding
and fixing homes, please visit
TheSystemToCash.com

More Books By the Author

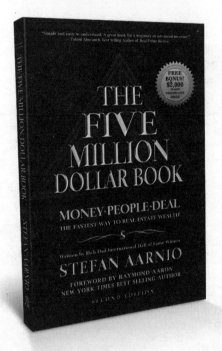

To Order, go to <u>TheFiveMillionDollarBook.com</u>

Stefan Aarnio is one of Canada's leading up and coming Real Estate Entrepreneurs and the winner of Canadian Real Estate Wealth Magazine's "Joint Venture Partner of the Year". Starting with only $1200, Stefan has built a multi million dollar portfolio for his partners and has earned himself a spot on The Self Made List. Stefan has accumulated properties at an alarming pace through his understanding of Real Estate Joint Ventures – The Fastest Way to Real Estate Wealth. Stefan's philosophy is simple, find great deals, build a fantastic team, pay everybody and create partnerships for life.

More Books By
The Author

What does it take to become a self-made millionaire? Many have wondered, few have succeeded. Self Made: Confessions of a Twenty Something Self Made Millionaire follows the real life story of Stefan Aarnio, award winning real estate investor and award winning entrepreneur through the struggle of starting out with zero cash, zero credit and zero experience in his pursuit of financial freedom. Inside Self Made, you will discover the 5 Secret Skills That Transform Ordinary People Into Self Made Millionaires. These skills are mastered by the rich, purposely not taught in school and are hidden from the poor and the middle class. Join Stefan on his journey as he faces financial ruin, meets his life-changing mentor and transforms his mind, body and soul to become Self Made.

Visit **SelfMadeConfessions.com** to order and receive your bonuses!

For a full list of products, please visit
stefanaarnio.com/store

To book speaking engagements with Stefan
please email **support@stefanaarnio.com**
or call **204-285-9882**

BLACKCARD UNIVERSITY

Real Estate Investing - Sales - Coaching

Are You Ready To Begin Your Journey To Total Freedom?

Join Blackcard University - A 5-year Wealth Building Curriculum

Blackcard University is different.
Get out of the classroom and inti the real world.
Get paid to learn by doing actual real estate deals.
Join Blackcard University's Mi5 Program and learn what it takes to
build wealth and become a millionaire in 5 years.

For more information, go to **blackcardu.com**